The Biggest Leap

Building a Profitable Insurance Agency from the Ground Up

By Timothy K. Gaspar

Table of Contents

Preface

Thank you, pops, for always believing in me.

Preface

I remember it like it was yesterday.

I drove to the courthouse in a truck that badly needed brakes (I am now an expert in how many times you can turn a rotor and what happens when you don't) and barely enough gas to get me home. My stepfather had paid my bankruptcy attorney because I could not, and my dad was too disappointed to speak to me.

Bankruptcy? But I am only 20 years old. I cannot legally buy beer and I am bankrupt? I do not have a college degree and I do not have a place to stay; and in the next few minutes, I will officially be filing for bankruptcy.

I have been an entrepreneur my whole life. I had lemonade stands, sold candy to other 6th graders, built a haunted house business in 9th grade, and bought a bunch of moon bounce houses for my 16th birthday. With those moon bounce houses, I started a decent sized rental company in high school and rented them along with cotton candy machines, sno-cone machines, and other party equipment. While most of my friends were at house parties, I spent most of my high school weekends schlepping around giant inflatables in my pickup truck. I thought I knew everything about, well, everything.

But there I was at 20 years old on the steps of that courthouse, learning the hard way what happens when you overextend yourself. I learned about the pitfalls of businesses without recurring revenue and the importance of having insurance if you are sued. I will spare you the details, but the end result was sitting in a bankruptcy court just before my 21st birthday.

This is a story about my own journey of entrepreneurship and the insurance business. I went from being bankrupt with no higher education and no direction to selling my business for tens of millions of dollars two months after my 40th birthday. What you will learn in this book is not some dumb get-rich-quick system about how to get leads without putting in effort. Instead, this book is a collection of lessons, habits, ideas, and hard-fought methodology that I have implemented successfully during my journey from my personal rock bottom through to the day I sold my insurance firm. It is true what they say, "if you think you can or think you can't, you are probably right."

Building your own insurance business, or any business for that matter, is not complicated. Creating your own business and brand is a lot of hard work, but it is not complicated. You do not need to know everything, and you do not have to make the perfect decision every time. The key is to master a few important principles - things that I happen to believe are truly necessary in business and in life. It has been said that "inspiration creates action," but I believe it is the consistent application of good habits that creates success. I hope you find a few habits and beliefs that you can adopt as your own to create the business and life that you want.

I wrote this book for only one reason: to help you build the insurance agency of your dreams. That's it. I know it sounds cheesy, but that is the truth. I am tired of seeing a growing number of charlatans, fakers, and social media "gurus" trying to sell insurance agents on systems, software programs, and training that promises quick money and immediate success. That is simply not the way this business works. These are the same social media characters who claim to have an amazing insurance business, but never actually disclose their agency revenue. They talk about a "million dollar agency," but they are referring to premium, not revenue. They do, however, have a great sales pitch designed to separate insurance agents and agency owners from their money. I wrote this book to tell you the truth and to tell you exactly what it takes to build an agency that generates millions of dollars in not only top line commission revenue but also profitability.

If you are reading this book, you are already the type of person who will be successful. You are making the investment in time and money (this book was not free) to learn. In this book, I will go over a lot of ideas - some of which you have probably heard before. Some ideas you will like and will be easy to run with. Other ideas you might think are silly and do not work for you, and that is fine. As I said, in business and in life, you don't need to get everything right; and what works for one person may not always work for another. You just need to get a few key things right by figuring out what works for you. I will talk several times in this book about the "pareto principal," which is the idea that 20% of your actions create 80% of your results.

As I will also say several times in this book, the insurance industry is a GREAT business. It is not without its frustrations, but it is still one of the best businesses in the world. We have no inventory to replenish or worry about spoiling, no machinery to buy, and no supply chain issues to worry about. What we do have is maybe the most wonderful business aspect: our revenue is recurring. Most importantly, though, we make a difference in people's lives. Once the fire trucks leave, once the panic of being served a lawsuit subsides, and once the casket of someone's loved one is closed, the topic will <u>always</u> shift to insurance and whether there is a policy to put your life or business back together.

In several areas of this book, I refer you to thebiggestleap.com for additional resources. Everything on that site is free and yours to use and share as you see fit. As you can imagine, writing a book aimed at insurance agents is going to sell more copies than a book about a child wizard from England so I have no need to monetize the website! That was thick sarcasm if you didn't get it; but honestly, I want to see you be successful more than I want to monetize my website. If you love the content, just buy me dinner one day when you are in Los Angeles.

I know I, for one, am guilty of sometimes starting a book, but not always finishing it. I ask that you read this book all the way through just in case one of the ideas (hopefully a lot more than one!) resonates with you, and you can put it into practice in your agency. I hope this book helps you build an amazing life for you and your family, and I wish you all the success and happiness imaginable.

Part 1: Building Your Book

Chapter 1: Ed

I believe there are a few reasons young people do not get into insurance.

#1: They do not usually know the industry exists.

#2: They do not see it as exciting, cool, or respectable.

#3: Most importantly, they do not see it as a career where they can do well or make a lot of money.

These reasons are doing this generation a tremendous disservice. Countless people could be making a significant amount of money doing something that truly can help others through some of the most difficult events in a person's life; but the media, particularly social media, show only a handful of careers.

The businesses that dominate media and are generally known or believed to make money are the flashier ones like athletes, entertainers, finance folks (meaning Wall Street types), attorneys, doctors, and influencers. The media tells young people a fictional tale about success being fast and flashy. One of the best lessons a young entrepreneur can learn is what really creates a great business and *how that is different from what other young people generally know or expect.*

If media does not introduce the youth to the insurance industry, then it is incumbent upon us to educate them and to show them the success that is possible through it. I had the good fortune to be introduce to insurance at a young age by my stepfather, Ed.

I grew up in a blended family environment. My parents divorced when I was three years old, and both my parents married wonderful people pretty quickly thereafter. My Dad married Jody, an amazingly sharp, young, future CFO; and my mom married Ed who would introduce me to the insurance business and teach me 99% of what I needed to know about this business.

It will sound silly, but the first thing I can remember about Ed was his Corvette. I must have been around five years old, and I still remember riding in his Corvette and how exciting the ride was. I would probably need to be in a space shuttle to recreate that feeling as an adult. My own dad was incredibly hard working and frugal and not really into flashy cars, his daily car was an Astro Van that was so many colors it looked more like an "Astro Pop". This Corvette though…. this was something! Ed was 26 when I met him and already had a Corvette, in addition to a Lincoln, a new house, and his third or fourth boat. All this to say, material things do not always point to how a person is doing financially; but when you are a kid, these are things that you notice.

The second thing I noticed about Ed is that he did not seem to work a lot. I do not mean he did not work hard or take work seriously. Rather, measured by the number of hours worked, he did not work as much as my Dad. My Dad was a workaholic (a trait I inherited), but I did not realize that at the time. What I saw were Ed's work schedule and his seemingly ample amount of free time. This is not a judgment of either work style, merely a study in contrasts.

Corvettes, boats, nice places - that was the theme of my first several years having Ed as my stepdad. I recall thinking "this guy does really well and seems to have a lot of time to vacation and enjoy weekends." As Ed's career progressed, the houses got bigger; and there were more cars, boats, trips, etc. As a child, I was always curious about business and what people did for work. I knew Ed sold insurance, and I saw that insurance must be a good business if Ed could provide this comfortable lifestyle.

And of course, insurance *is* a good business. In fact, as I mentioned before and will surely mention again, insurance is a *great* business. My childhood was influenced by witnessing a man who loved what he did for a living enjoy his life and the spoils of doing well in his work.

Watching Ed, I got to see what made a great salesperson, which is "step one" in building a great insurance agency. This, however, is not a sales book. This is a book about how to create an amazing insurance agency, and being a great salesperson is just the first and most essential step of many.

There are a myriad qualities that can make someone successful at sales; but in Ed's case, if I had to distill his skillset down to one word, it would be: **relationships**.

You may have heard the adage that you end up being the average of the five people you hang out with the most. If you hang out with people who like to party and drink all weekend, you will end up doing that too much. If you hang out with people who eat too much, do not exercise, and are overweight, that will be you too. The same is true on the other side. If you hang out with people who are successful and do well in life, that too will be you.

Ed cultivated relationships with people who would ultimately help his career. Ed always surrounded himself with people more successful than he. Hanging out with people more successful, smarter, more generous, or interesting than you see yourself will push you to be a better version of yourself. Many times, unfortunately, we see the opposite where someone will hang out with people less successful in order to feel good about themselves. Not Ed though. Ed sought out people who were already where he wanted to be. That was the key in helping him get there.

Ed was not the only person who benefited from these relationships. As a child and young adult, I got to see up close what made these people so successful. They may not have gone to the best schools, but they continued to educate themselves and learn, driven to be better and do better. This group had common sense; drive and focus; and, most importantly, had a positive mindset.

That last piece, the positive mindset, probably accounts for 99% of your future results. It does not matter what you do or how you do it. If you do not believe that you will be successful, then you are predicting the future. It is perfectly fine to doubt yourself sometimes or to fear failure; but at the end of the day, you must believe that you will be successful and stay positive. Remember that life is not fair, and *everyone* will be dealt a different hand in life. *Everyone* will face challenges. *Everyone* at some point will experience heart break, disappointment, loss, pain, fear, and sadness. What makes the difference between the high achiever and the low achiever is how they deal with those negative emotions and how they move forward.

To that last point on positive thinking, I have met many people over the years who are in insurance who do not do very well financially. One of my first jobs after my bankruptcy was as an agent in a small property & casualty agency in California. The agency had seven or eight seasoned agents when I joined.

I remember how shocked I was when these agents I encountered would talk badly about the insurance business, would complain they were not paid enough, would complain there were not enough leads, would complain about their clients, and on and on. If not for complaining, these people would not have anything to talk about! I walked into the same office years after they did with the same products, the same lead opportunities, the same carriers, and the same software. Yet, there they were stagnant with the same complaints years later when I left that agency to start my own agency. What made the difference between me and them was that I had the belief that I was starting my adventure in a great business, and that made all the difference.

> "Your talent determines what you can do. Your motivation determines how much you are willing to do. Your attitude determines how well you do it."
>
> – Lou Holtz

You probably would not have bought this book if you had a crappy attitude. Honestly, if your attitude is negative, there is nothing I can say in this book to help you. On the flipside, with a positive attitude, you are going to have success; but there are some specific items you need to know to build a great insurance agency.

Chapter 2: Relationships and Prospecting

As I mentioned in Chapter 1, a key part of Ed's success was relationships. For me, that was and still is a huge part of my business and life. What exactly are relationships though? To get started, let's talk about what relationships are *not*.

Relationships are <u>not</u> connections on LinkedIn. Relationships are not "friends" on social media or "likes" on your posts. Relationships are not people on your newsletter email list. Anybody who wants to sell you on building your own insurance book solely using LinkedIn, social media, and email is full of crap. People who reach out to you on social media are not having success in their business, and generally they are afraid to reach out in real life. Don't be that person!

Prospecting is *the* thing. It is the thing that separates someone who independently builds a successful insurance book (or any professional sales related business) from someone who struggles in sales and ultimately must remain an employee working for someone else. At the end of the day, prospecting is the ability to create your own leads and opportunities through relationships. Notice that it is to *create* your own leads, not *buy* your own leads. I do not personally believe in buying leads, but that is from experience. I have done it, and it has never led to positive growth. Leads that you buy are typically price shoppers who do not know or trust you. They are getting hounded by dozens of insurance agents at the same time. As a consumer, I think your phone number being on a lead list sold to countless insurance agents is tied with being on a lead list about the expiration of your extended warranty as the cruelest things that can happen in life!

Since leads are essentially useless, knowing how to prospect is the single most valuable skill you can have as an agent. If you are not a great closer but are a good prospector, you can more than make up for the former by getting more into your pipeline. Get more "at bats," and you will get more chances at closing. Ultimately with practice, you will get better at closing.

On the flip side, if you are a great closer but do not know how to prospect, you will end up working somewhere that gives you leads. This is because you are never going to be able to close if you do not have leads from which to sell. <u>Someone who knows how to prospect is going to make</u>

<u>many multiples more than the person who only knows how to close.</u>

Prospecting is where the value is. Companies spend huge amounts of their annual budgets trying to get clients in the door and will pay handsomely to someone with the skill to bring new customers in.

Prospecting through relationships is the key to your success as an agent. Many agents start their careers cold calling, which, as you may know from experience, is hard. I do want to mention here, however, that cold calling is actually *easier* than it was twenty years ago. Agents now have a variety of ways to prospect cold leads other than an uncomfortable call; and of course, most agents will pick the less uncomfortable option.

As I mentioned a moment ago, most agents will post on social media, message people on LinkedIn, send hundreds or thousands of emails, and attend meetings of local networking groups. What they will not do is pick up the phone and call total strangers. Or even better, even fewer still will cold call a business in person. 99.9% will not take the initiative to make that connection in person, but doing it does make you stand out. The same is true with knocking on doors. Whether it's households or businesses, very few insurance agents are out knocking on doors so if you do, you will get noticed.

With that all being said, I recognize that cold calling and door knocking are awkward and difficult. In prospecting, the warmer the lead, the better. Warm leads come from relationships. I want to share with you one of the most important tools you can have as an insurance agent - it's a yellow pad on your desk with the words "Lunch List" written at the top. This list is comprised of the prospects or centers of influence who know lots of other people. The goal of this list is <u>not</u> to sell these people. The goal is to take them for a bite to eat to get to know them better and create a meaningful relationship. As you get closer to people on a personal level, they will eventually come on as your clients as long as they know the door is open to them. The more genuine the relationship is and the less you are "in it" for your own benefit, the more you will gain both professionally and also personally.

In any new relationship, try to gauge in the first meeting if the relationship will go anywhere based on how much you like the person. That's right - <u>do not</u> gauge the relationship on financial opportunity or connections. Base it on how much you like the person. If you like someone, it is probably because you found things in common, and surprise - that person probably likes you too! People want to do business with people they like; and honestly, trying to build a relationship with someone you do not like or enjoy spending time with is just plain hard.

For the people you really hit it off with, the goal is to expand that relationship by meeting friends and associates of that person. Again, it's birds of a feather. When you meet someone that turns out to be your ideal client, you want to meet their closest associates. As I mentioned above, people tend to be the average of the top five people they hang out with. You want to be part of that crowd.

So, where do you start? Anywhere! Any opportunity to see someone in person is a win. When you are getting started, the idea is to get in front of as many people as possible with the goal of in-person one-on-ones, which includes breakfast, lunch, coffee, etc. It doesn't matter what the reason is as long as you get one-on-one time to build a relationship. The one-on-one aspect is key. I have seen professional salespeople spend countless hours hopping between multiple business networking groups, chambers of commerce, and other group meetings only to complain that they did not get any business. Nobody is going to meet you at an event for the first time and then give you a bunch of business! They do not know you! The idea is to meet people you hit it off with at events and then invite them to lunch or coffee to start building a relationship. I do not mean a relationship built on you expecting business. If you start relationships that way, the other person will smell that salesy scent from a mile away. I mean <u>real</u> relationships!

As you cultivate more and more relationships, the ones that will flourish are the ones that are real. There are people you will genuinely like hanging out with and eventually that will turn into business. Every meaningful relationship you create with another human being has value. You will not always know what it is up front, but the value will always be there. Perhaps the value is greater for the other party in the relationship, and that is okay. The question is not how a relationship can benefit you today; the question is how a relationship can be meaningful to both parties over a lifetime. Keep this question in your mind at the beginning of every encounter.

For newer relationships where you are first getting to know someone, try to give more than they do and try to give first, if you can. Obviously, pay for lunch or that beer, and see how you can help that person personally or in business.

The need for humans to reciprocate a favor is huge, and most people will feel very uncomfortable until they can return a favor (hopefully a referral) to you. If you cannot provide someone a favor, you can send them a book they might enjoy with a handwritten note or an introduction to someone that might help their career. Listen deeply to the other person, their interests, goals, hobbies, etc. and you will always find ways to do something special for them without it costing much at all. People who take a genuine interest in helping others are rare. Be that person.

With all that being said, where exactly do you meet prospects? The folks you meet at chamber of commerce meetings and networking events are great, but what about the "low hanging fruit?" Think about your neighbors, high school and college classmates, cousins, and old co-workers. When was the last time you invited them to coffee or for a drink? Re-kindle and/or show interest in the relationship and casually see how you can help them in their own lives if there is an opportunity. People do business with people they like.

This is where some agents get weird about handling insurance for people they know. I met a few agents over the years who were adamant about not having friends and family as clients. I am not sure where some agents come up with the "rule" that you are not supposed to have family and friends as clients, but that is not a good rule to follow because you are cutting off your potential at its knees. I have never met a massively successful agent who did not have their closest family and friends as clients. Aside from your relationship with them, wouldn't you want to be able to help your friend or family member in a stressful time in their life?

There is, of course, no need to be pushy. If a friend or family member does not want to do business with you for whatever reason, get over it and do not take it personally. As much as I believe your friends and family should do business with you, I do not believe you should hold it against someone if they choose otherwise. For me, somewhere around 80-90% of my friends and family are clients, but I still love the 10-20% who are not. As long as my family and friends know what I do, that is good enough for me.

The goal in managing relationships is to have as many positive relationships as you can actively manage. In many cases, you will take on the role of the "relationship manager." The reality is that in most friendships, one friend has to be the one to take action to get together by initiating contact. A lot of people simply are not wired to do the work needed to keep a relationship active, even if they really enjoy your company. It is not usually intentional; people are just busy, and life happens. Look at your role as the person to keep the relationship going; the other person will appreciate it even if they do not say so. If you are the person who always has to reach out to that high school buddy or if, maybe, you are the one who always has to arrange that poker game for your high school buddies, then you are the "relationship manager." You are the glue that keeps people together, and it is a role in which everyone benefits from your efforts. This role also gives you influence over any group; and in sales, being the group influencer is *exactly* where you want to be.

As you become busier with more relationships, you need to establish a system to juggle them. I started with that "lunch list" on a yellow pad I mentioned earlier. This list is the people who are clients, old friends, or leaders in the community who are prospects or centers of influence who know lots of other people. I would track the last time I grabbed a bite with them. Over time, I switched to a spreadsheet that is more trackable, searchable, and allows me to create fields for how I know them, their interests, and their addresses for personal holidays cards and things like that.

In addition to a tracking mechanism, nurturing relationships takes time, which is something none of us have enough of. How can you find the time to make sure you are staying in front of people? Well, for one, never eat breakfast or lunch alone. We are all busy, and eating a meal while busily working at your desk is always tempting, but resist the urge. You have two distinct opportunities each day to spend time with someone and build a real relationship so do not waste it returning emails with one hand and munching on a sandwich in the other.

Secondly, you have some events and rituals you already do in your life that are social in nature. Do you typically host a Super Bowl party? What a great opportunity to invite people you want to get to know better! If you have not previously hosted a Super Bowl party, maybe you should! Is your 3-year-old daughter having a birthday? Great! Maybe invite some of your clients or prospective clients with kids the same age. My Dad always had a weekly poker night, Monday Night Football get-togethers, hiking groups, etc. I grew up watching Ed blend personal and business relationships and watched him keep dozens of friends over many decades. Cultivating and nurturing your relationships takes work, but it is work that creates tremendous return on investment not only in business, but in your personal life as well.

I did not fully appreciate the importance of this until I saw that other insurance agents and other professionals drew an imaginary line between personal and business relationships. I know that some people are uncomfortable with the idea of inviting a client into your home, but you need to get over that because trust and a personal bond will pay dividends in both your work and your satisfaction and happiness in life.

In case you still do not believe me, I want to give two quick examples of business relationships making an indelible impact on life. My first example is my friend Doug. Doug was an agent at that agency I started working at early in my insurance career. As a mentor to me, Doug and I became fast friends, working on many cases together and socializing after work and on weekends. What started as a business relationship turned into a deep and meaningful friendship over the past couple decades. In 2022 when my friend Doug needed a kidney, I was more than happy to volunteer to be tested; and unbelievably I was a complete match to donate to Doug!

Doug and I had not worked together since 2008, but the friendship we created before that was genuine. In the time between 2008 and 2022, we both put in the effort to remain friends. Just think if I had lost contact with Doug after I left that job. I would not have had the blessing of being there for Doug when it mattered the most. Trust me, the blessing was all mine (by the way Doug's body accepted the kidney and he is doing fantastic!).

My second example was the support I got when my father passed away suddenly in a mountain bike accident, also in 2022. This was easily the most painful event of my life. If you have experienced the loss of your parent, then you can understand. I was simply overwhelmed by the number of business contacts and customers who reached out to me and my family with their condolences, flowers, gifts, and hugs during that time. It was amazing and made me realize the importance of every relationship - even those that are based more on "business" than "personal." The reality is there is no difference between a "personal relationship" and a "business relationship" and one key to your success will be your ability to turn personal friends into clients and vice versa.

On a separate note, do not overlook the people who became clients quickly before you get a chance to know them. New clients can present one of your best opportunities to forge a relationship with someone great. There are a couple of reasons new clients are great to hang out with on a personal level. First, as you grow the relationship, that person will introduce you as their insurance agent because that is how you met. Having a third party introduce you as "their insurance agent" gives you the identity of insurance agent and, in most cases, you are not what they pictured as an insurance agent. When people picture an insurance agent, they often picture a nerdy, boring, out of shape bald white guy. So, if you are a minority, female or more athletic, this will throw the person for a little bit of a loop and that is a good thing. And, if you are indeed an out of shape balding white guy then you should probably get started on your personality.

The other reason to cultivate relationships with your new clients is because it lets the clients know that you truly value them. The client will know you already got their business so you are not taking them to a baseball game just to get their business because you already have it. Instead you must truly value them and/or their business.

Professional salespeople who stay in touch after the initial sale experience the most success. It is a common thread among top performers in insurance, real estate, politics, etc. Just a quick tip, your city probably has a local business journal or local paper that highlights people in your community. When you see your clients highlighted or mentioned, cut out the article or their picture and send it to them with a personal note congratulating them. Everyone likes to be noticed for something positive and this will go a long way to cement your relationship with them.

Keeping your focus on the relationship piece is a no-lose proposition. Life is richer with great relationships, and great relationships will literally make you richer.

Chapter 3: Dress the Part

When did the "insurance bro" style become a thing? I have been watching these "insurance experts" on YouTube sell other agents on how to be successful, and they are always wearing a backwards hat and a t-shirt. Nobody wants to get advice from someone dressed like a character from "Jay and Silent Bob."

Dressing in a professional way is critically important. The first reason: it tells your client and the world that you respect them and respect yourself. The second reason: it affects how you think! For me, at least, putting on even just slacks and a dress shirt makes me feel more capable as a businessperson. I know, I know! That sounds so stupid, but it is true! I notice a difference in my own abilities when wearing cargo shorts (yes, I still own those) and wearing a suit and tie.

My entire career I have always worn a tie. When I first started in 2001, this was more commonplace than now. Nowadays, I get comments about my tie nearly everyday. Sometimes it is a compliment (I think Starbucks training includes a rule about always complimenting a customer's tie), sometimes it is a jab or joke at my expense, or sometimes it is someone mistaking me for an employee for just about every retail establishment I walk into. No matter the comment, I love it! Dressing sharp and, in my case, wearing a tie are noticeable. Are ties outdated? Maybe, but that is not the point. <u>The point is not about looking cool and stylish. It is about standing out and being successful.</u> What is your goal every day? Is your goal to be in GQ magazine? Good for you, but that will not make you likeable. Dress like someone who is serious about what they do, and you will attract that type of client.

I have talked specifically about ties, but my point is to always dress a little nicer than your client or your audience will be dressed. If you are going to visit a manufacturing plant or tire shop, then do not wear a tie because that will alienate your customer. If you are going to visit a CPA or attorney office where many people might have ties, wear a suit and tie. Just dress one level up from the "norm." You will present more professionally, more seriously, and be that much more distinctive.

Chapter 4: The Importance of Follow Up

After prospecting, following up is probably the second most important skill for you and your business going forward. You can get a lot of things wrong in this business, but still do well if you master the art of following up.

If you are in this business, you must accept the fact that people do not like insurance. I am sorry to break that to you, but have you noticed your insurance stories do not exactly kill it at cocktail parties? And what do most people do with any subject they do not like? That's right - they avoid it!

Your prospective clients know they need to buy that insurance policy they spoke to you about, but they do not like it and they do not want to think about it. 99% of the time your prospective customer is not in the mood to think about insurance, let alone buy it. You must continue to follow up until you just happen to reach them during that moment during the day when they are open to talking about and maybe even buying the insurance they know they need. You really do have to catch the buyer "in the mood."

Statistics show most buyers must be asked for the sale nine times before saying yes. Every time you make a follow up call, remind yourself it is one more call of the nine you will need to get the sale. Do not feel discouraged when you get the first "no" or even the second. You will probably need to call seven or eight more times. From the client's perspective, every time you call is an opportunity to show consistency in your personality and work ethic, and you will set yourself apart with your follow-up tenacity alone.

It is critical to make your follow-ups a daily habit to be addressed at the start of your day. Do not check your emails first. Do not download that new software program. Do not refill your coffee cup until those calls are done. Treat your follow-up calls like you have a phone call with the President, the Pope, or one of your kids. I remember having dozens of quotes spread all over my desk, and I would call them in some cases dozens of times until they bought or told me to drop dead. I never needed to be pushy. If the person was not ready, then I would simply call them again in a week and the week after that. Eventually I would catch them on the right day. It was not a matter of being a "closer" or "saying the right thing." It was a matter of consistency and not giving up. Grit will win over high pressure every time. Every follow-up call you make builds that muscle for you and makes it much easier to make more follow-up calls. In some ways, it is easier to make fifty follow up calls in a day than five.

When it comes to follow-up and most communication for that matter, remember that email sucks. Sure, email is useful for some types of communication, but honestly email is over-utilized in just about every insurance operation I have ever seen. Email is not a sales tool. Email is good for two things: scheduling and confirmation.

Likewise, I have never been a big fan of texting. For some reason it always felt more intrusive to me, but you must do what works for you. Calling your prospects is much more uncomfortable than emailing or texting, but that is the same for everyone. In sales, it is always best to do what is most uncomfortable because it sets you apart from the rest.

A couple final notes about following up. Every time you talk to the customer, they are telling you valuable things about themselves so be sure to take notes. Perhaps the customer is telling you about where their children go to school or excitedly mentions their tickets to the Rams game.

Mention these things in the follow-ups without seeming like a creep. This shows the prospect that you know how to listen and that you care about them, not just them as a sale.

Lastly, even when a prospect gives you an emphatic "no," calendar the follow-up call for next year. Next year always comes sooner than you think. Some of your best cases will come two or even three years later if it's more complicated or commercial insurance. The prospect will again be impressed that you followed through. By that time, they also may be disenchanted with the incumbent agent or whoever they went with instead of you; and you are catching them at the right time.

Chapter 5: Don't Water the Weeds

What do you think when you look outside and see weeds starting to sprout up in your beautiful garden? Do you rush outside to water the weeds and give them special plant food to grow taller? Of course not! You pull the weeds and make sure they do not take over your garden. Unfortunately, most agents treat their home gardens better than their book of business, allowing the weeds to flourish and choke out the flowers.

You have heard the story before: an insurance agent is complaining about the client who always calls their cell phone at 10 pm on a Sunday about a $5 bill. The agent tells the story partly for sympathy and partly to brag about their dedication to their job as insurance agent. How incredibly stupid! Every time you take a call from "that" insured, you are saying "hey, it is perfectly acceptable to call me anytime you want about anything you want. My time has no value, and I do not want to spend time with my family. And please, tell your friends who act like you that I would love to have them as clients."

Okay, that is a little over the top, but not really. Every time you take that call, you are encouraging that behavior from that client; and that client really will refer you the same types of folks. "Birds of a feather" remember! Outside of business hours, you are allowed to not answer your phone, you are allowed to ask customers to call the office, you are allowed to screen your calls. The idea that customers will fire you for not being there on a Sunday afternoon for a billing call is a story you have told yourself that is mostly fiction. And if that customer does fire you, then that is a win for you.

If you try to be 24/7 for every client, you will burn out and burn out fast. That is the reality of it. The truth of the matter that nobody likes to admit is that it feels good to take that call, to be needed, to be dependable. Unfortunately, in our business, that way of doing business can drown you quickly with too many clients expecting you to answer billing questions on Thanksgiving.

Set boundaries with your clients. Most will respect the boundaries and respect you. If you never take calls on a Sunday night, then nobody will expect you to do so. Here is the best part: some clients will, in fact, get upset that you are not at their beck and call and will leave for another agent, and that's great! You just killed the weed and stopped more from popping up. Please do not misunderstand me! I <u>love</u> great customer service, but there is a difference between creating a great customer service journey and creating a situation that is not scalable and sure to burn you out.

One other note about watering the "weeds." Sometimes the "weeds" do not look like weeds. Sometimes they are customers who create far more service than their policy revenue justifies. A good example would be the average small general contractor. The premium may look decent at an $8,000 premium, but this general contractor calls you weekly for certificates and they are always a rush. Of course, when it comes time to pay the insurance bill, it is not so much of a rush. These customers will demand far more service and its corresponding service costs than the revenue it is worth.

What matters is not the revenue on an account, but rather the revenue divided by the number of "touches" the account requires. An account that generates $300 in revenue, but requires no servicing (like a direct bill lessors risk policy for example) has far more value than a high service policy that generates $800 in commission (like that contractor).

Well, this chapter title makes about as much sense as the statement "wherever you go, there you are" which, of course, is also true, but obvious. The funny thing, though, is how many people are not themselves everywhere they go. I have noticed that who some people are varies depending on their situation or environment.

For some people, there is a defined boundary between their work life and their personal life, and that is a boundary they are not comfortable crossing. I remember a conversation with my client Don, who is a very successful businessman and one of the best salespeople I have ever seen. Don went from being a salesperson in the food business to owning a very successful produce distribution business. Don recounted bumping into his CPA at a party. While other people were mingling and having a good time, Don asked the CPA a question about a recent tax law change and what it meant. The CPA was taken aback by the question, "Whoa, this is a party. I can't answer any tax questions right now. Call me Monday."

I do not know how much Don spent with this CPA, but it certainly was not a $300 tax return. We are most certainly talking about tens of thousands of dollars annually, if not more. With that one statement, the CPA was almost saying, "Hey, that's the *other* me that only exists Monday through Friday during the day." Needless to say, the CPA did not have to worry about Don asking him tax questions at parties for much longer. Don made a switch to someone who is a CPA all the time.

The question is: are you who you say you are?

If you are an advisor, then you are an advisor. When people count on you for advice, that matters all the time - not just when you are in the mood. From a marketing standpoint, you want people to always see you as the insurance person. If you show up at a wedding, a party, or a funeral, you want people to say, "Hey, that's John the insurance guy." Even better, you want people to introduce you as "Samantha, my insurance agent." What better marketing could you have? If this is what you do, then go "all in," be proud of what you do and the value it brings to clients, and never turn it "off." This same point can obviously be made for character. If you are the type of person who cuts a lot of corners in their personal life, then people will assume you do that professionally, and they are probably right.

You are one person - be the same person everywhere you go.

Part II: From Book to Business

The first part of this book talked about the principles I personally have used and have seen other successful agents use to build their book of business. For some, that is enough and they will be perfectly satisfied. Honestly, focusing on just being an amazing agent is admirable. You will do fantastic financially, and you will have a lot less headaches than someone building a company. For others, however, they feel a need to be take *the biggest leap* from the safety of being a stellar agent to becoming an entrepreneur and building their own agency. In my experience, you are either one or the other. If you decide to start an agency only for the possible financial gain, then your chances are not great. I will explain.

Building any business, including an insurance business, is exceptionally difficult. Even if you are a great salesperson or maybe even especially if you are a great salesperson (more on that in a moment), building a business is significantly different than building a *book* of business.

The skills that make you an amazing salesperson are not the same skills that will make you an amazing sales manager or agency owner. The skills you will need in building systems and operations are different than those we discussed in the first half of this book, although there is certainly some overlap. Once an entrepreneur, important pieces like relationships and maintaining boundaries with clients are even more important. The challenges and headaches involved in starting your own agency can sometimes be enough for many people to throw in the towel if they only started it solely for the money. You have to really want it to succeed and to succeed big.

If you have a "fire in your belly" to start an insurance agency or to build your current agency, then you are going to do this no matter what. Maybe your motivation is leaving a legacy, maybe you want to give other people opportunity, or maybe you need to show up the people who said you were going to fail. Whatever your motivation is, as long as you are dedicated, focused, persistent, and willing to continue learning every day, then you are going to do amazingly well.

Chapter 7: The Biggest Leap

And here we are, the chapter that shares this book's name. There are other, later chapters that have much more value with regard to discussing skills like building relationships or specific tactics that will help you build a successful agency operation. This chapter is not that. Rather, this chapter is about exactly what the title implies - taking your biggest leap. The reason this chapter is so important is because if you do not take this step, nothing else matters. You can be the world's best salesperson, an amazing people manager, and have a mind designed for creating business systems; but if you do not take *the biggest leap,* you will be using those skills making someone else a lot of money.

I remember sitting at a bank in Studio City, CA in early 2008, where I had just opened my business bank account for my fledgling insurance agency. I had refinanced my house to get the $225,000 I needed to buy my book of business from the agency for whom I worked. That agency allowed me to "vest" in my book and do a buyout, and I had been planning out my business plan for almost a year. This, however, was the moment of truth. I was asking the bank to make a $200,000 cashier's check out to my old agency so I could leave and take the leap to start my own agency. I thought seriously about just getting in my car and not taking the leap. I thought seriously about staying comfortable in my lane where I knew I could be successful being someone else's employee.

Something, however, held me down in that bank's chair and told me to follow through. I held that cashier's check in my hand and promptly delivered it to my old agency to buy my book of business.

I would say delivering the news to my old boss that I was leaving his agency was the hardest part of the leap, but it was in fact the second hardest part. The hardest part of the process was the subsequent two weeks when my old boss offered me incentive after incentive to stay: a commission split increase, a car allowance, and even some ownership percentage in his agency.

I am so thankful in hindsight that I did not take him up on any of those things. I knew I had what it took to start my own agency and to be as successful, if not much more so, as I was there. *Do not settle.* Making difficult decisions and choosing a challenge in life are what create the most fulfillment and happiness, so have the confidence to move forward. That is what I did.

Taking the leap to go out on your own is the key thing that separates the dreamers from the doers. I am not the best at any of the things I talk about in this book. I have met many people who are better salespeople, planners, managers, and strategists than I; but those people had either no interest or no willingness to take the leap in going out on their own. Taking a leap of faith and trusting only yourself is difficult for a few reasons.

I think the biggest reason people decide not to become entrepreneurs is fear of the unknown. The fear that you will not have what it takes to be successful and that you will let down all the people who love you (more on those people in a second). The thing to remember when you hit this mental hurdle is that the future is unknown regardless. Your current boss might be thinking about doing a layoff right now and you are not aware. Your current agency may be in the process of selling and you will not find out until a new name is on the door. The sense of safety a person has in working for someone else is an illusion, one that will leave you always wondering what could have been.

After fear, one of the biggest reasons people do not take the big leap is family and loved ones, but maybe not in the way you think. It is not the fear of being unable to provide for your family (although that will certainly be a massive motivator). It is the fear of disapproval. People who love you will not want you to take the big leap. People who love you do not want you to get hurt, and they generally will prefer you play it safe or, at least, what is safe in their mind. Going against your family's advice can be incredibly difficult and emotional, particularly with the potential for having them disapprove of your choice. Starting a business can be a lonely endeavor, but it will create massive opportunity for your entire family one day in the future.

In my case, I *had* to be an entrepreneur. It was and is my identity. For the second time in my life, six years after my personal bankruptcy, I was an entrepreneur again. I had my ducks mostly in a row at that point. I had office space, a customer service person on board (who lasted two whole weeks!), my agency management system in place, and a contract with a "cluster" to place my business with carriers. I had been thinking about how to make my agency successful incessantly for the past year and most certainly before that. I would offer my customers cold drinks, fancy espresso, and snacks when they came in. I would send birthday cards and holiday cards with a lotto ticket scratcher. I would only hire the world's most amazing customer service people. I had some of my best ideas while working for someone else because I saw what I did not want to do. That's not a dig on the agency I worked for, but I wanted to be different. I wanted to be better.

As I just mentioned as a key step, I had been planning this leap for a while. My business plan was far from perfect, but I had one. I talk about the importance of a plan because I watched other people start insurance agencies before me that did not last very long. You have likely heard the statistic that 90% of businesses fail in their first five years; but the truth is that if you factor in only those businesses that started with a business plan (even a short, simple one), the rate of success is much higher.

Starting a business takes planning and flexibility. As a new agency owner, you are probably going to be doing almost every role on day one. The person who answers the phone? That's you. The person who does the accounting? That's you. The person who sets up your computer and handles the IT? That's you. You do not need to be an expert in these things, but you do need a plan for getting all these jobs done. That first customer service person I hired lasted two whole weeks so for a little while I was not only the recruiter for a new account manager, but I was also my own customer service person.

This planning piece is important to understand. "Taking the biggest leap" without a plan is like jumping out of a plane without a parachute.

As I mentioned, this section of the book is about starting a business, not continuing to build your own book of a business. The distinction you need to make is whether you want to build a "lifestyle business," which is a business where you bring home as much as possible (both income and vacation hours) to maximize your personal lifestyle, or a "long-term business" designed to run well into the future, even without you. My goal was to build the long-term business, and most of my advice and my own story will center around that. I will mention that most business owners, especially those in the insurance business, are more "lifestyle" business owners.

Being focused on long term growth means you will make different decisions and make certain short-term sacrifices that lifestyle businesses do not have to make. On the flip side, the long term business will give you many opportunities that the lifestyle business cannot. The potential financial incentives are far greater with a long term business than a lifestyle business as long as you are patient.

First things first: you have to realize you are no longer just an insurance agent, you are also a business owner. If you grow big enough, you will no longer be an insurance agent at all; you will be a CEO. That latter part is an important distinction some agency owners never make.

You have to work _on_ your business, not _in_ your business.

If you adopt the mindset of being the agent for all customers and new business, then you will never be able to scale and you will end up stalled in an office with a handful of people. You might make great money; and if you enjoy being an agent running your small business, then that is great! But, if your dreams are bigger than that, you need to think differently.

Your day-to-day goal as a true entrepreneur growing a long term business is to put yourself out of a job. You need to grow enough to hire a receptionist so you don't need to answer the phone. You need to grow enough to hire an accounting person in-house so you do not need to do the accounting. You need to grow enough to hire an IT person. You need to grow enough to hire salespeople so you do not need to make all the sales. You get the point.

Every time you hire someone to do a job that you were previously doing, you free up your own time to work on the business. This allows you time to look for the best people, to think of great marketing campaigns, and to create systems that allow your business to thrive. Once you have a business that is humming along without your daily interaction, you now have something you can sell; or at least something that can provide income to you while you are on an island somewhere with the people you love if that is your goal.

One thing to be aware of in taking your leap, remember I mentioned that taking the leap without a plan is like jumping out of a plane without a parachute? Well, even with a plan, your parachute probably will not open right away. At first you might feel like you are freefalling. You will work more hours for less pay, things that you never thought about before (like trust accounting!) now take up your nights and weekends. This is just part of the leap, and I promise you that if you stick with it your parachute will open.

Whatever your plan is and wherever you want to go, begin with the end in mind. Most people overestimate what they can do in a year but underestimate what they can do in five or ten years. When you think of where you want your firm to be, why not think big? The 10 largest brokerages in the world have between $2.8 billion and $20 billion in annual revenue - why not shoot for that? Most of the very large agencies and insurance operations you see today similarly started as tiny one or two person shops. As an example, the world's largest brokerage, Arthur J. Gallagher, started as a two man shop fifty years ago. Today Gallagher is at $8 billion in revenue.

Very few industries offer you the opportunity to scale to this level. As another example, in 2020, the revenue for insurance-giant Marsh McLennan exceeded that of McDonalds. What other business can start as a one to two man shop and grow into a billion-dollar business within a single lifetime? If you are lucky enough to be in this industry, I think insurance is the best industry in the world. Remember the opportunity

for you and that your business has no limits.
Dream big.

Chapter 8: Full Time Clients Only

There are literally dozens of metrics that you can measure for your agency to track how you are doing: new production, sales velocity, retention, loss ratio, revenue per employee, net promoter score, etc. Those numbers are all important for different reasons; but one metric in particular will show you how your agency is doing - *average account size.*

If you handle a lot of small monoline accounts, it is going to be hard to make money. The amount of time it takes to handle a $10,000 revenue (not premium) account is not 10x the amount of work it takes to handle a $1,000 revenue account. In fact, in some cases the $1,000 revenue account is more work, and in many cases a $100 revenue account is the most work! Remember when we talked about the "weeds" earlier - I should have mentioned that most of the weeds are not very tall.

This does not mean you need to focus your agency on the largest commercial accounts. In fact, unless you have a specialty (more on that later), focusing on the largest commercial accounts might have you competing with big national brokerages, which is not something you want to do (at least not right off the bat). The idea is to make sure that you get all of the possible business from every client you have.

Let me be clear though. This does not mean to sell policies that the insured does not need. First, that is a sure-fire way to get a crummy reputation. Second, it is obviously unethical. What I mean is that you should try to be the insurance agent for your clients on all the policies they need. For your average personal lines account, policies like auto, home (or renters), and life insurance are a necessity. For those with assets to protect, there should always be an umbrella in place, as well as policies specific to certain geographical areas like earthquake insurance for California or wind coverage for Florida. You get the idea. Ensuring your clients have all the appropriate policies to get them covered and ensuring you are the agent on all of them is the key. If you can get the policies to have one concurrent effective date, even better as it is more manageable and less complicated for the insured and less work for your team with one renewal review to do instead of several.

Ensuring you are the only insurance agency for each of your clients is obviously your goal already, so why is it hard to only take on full time clients? The hard part is saying no.

When a client says they are only going to give you a single policy or you are one of two or more agencies on a single customer, your agency has to say no. The most important piece of this is ensuring your team practices this, and you as the leader must enforce these types of practices. Your agents will want to write anyone with a heartbeat. Although they want the entire account on any customer, they are not going to walk away from an account unless they fully buy into your agency's full-time client-only strategy and know that is the rule. To an agent any sale is a "win", it is your job as a leader to set the tone on which "wins" actually count.

This is one of many areas where getting your team to go along with your strategy will need to be measured and managed. If you say you are a "full time client only" agency but you do not audit your files and new accounts, your agents will nod in agreement and then make exceptions most of the time. You must ensure you audit both new business and renewals to confirm your clients have all their insurance with you.

Auditing new accounts does not have to be fancy or time consuming. The goal is to ensure the new accounts coming into the agency are the types of accounts you want and are indeed "full time." Ensure your producers know exactly what that means and what the expectations are on rounding out accounts. If a producer writes only one piece of business but promises they will round out the account soon, then there must be a plan.

When will the producer round out the account? Who are the other policies with now? Every producer must have a well thought out plan on how they will round out accounts that are not yet rounded out.

When you find that agents or team members are not following your rules, do not tolerate it even if, or even *especially*, for big producers. You get what you tolerate. Enforce your agency guidelines early and always to set your culture. When a producer writes a monoline account, there is no need to fire the account. Just make it a "house" account. Thank the producer for their donation to your "house" book and do not budge on giving the account back. You only need to do that a couple of times before the producers stop writing monoline accounts.

Knowing your average account size will allow you to systematize a certain level of service to make sure you keep the business. If you have monoline policies worth an average of $150 in annual commission, how much service can you give them? Not much. If your average personal lines client generates $600 a year in commission however, you _can_ afford to do more. Perhaps a birthday card with a lottery ticket to every client on their birthday? We do that, and they are the best marketing dollars we spend, hands down. How about a pint of ice cream with your logo to your client after an accident? Would that make your customers say "wow!"? You bet it would. Most importantly, how about making sure your clients get an annual review every year or at least an attempt to do so? You can only do those things if each account generates enough revenue to cover your costs and generate a profit. Having full time clients will impact your average account value more than any other activity.

For personal lines, a full time client also includes the life insurance piece. If you are a property and casualty agent, I bet you agree that life insurance is a necessity. I also bet you sell very little of it. I may be wrong and you may be the exceptional P & C agent who also does huge life production, but that is rare. The only reason this is rare is because P & C agents do not ask about life insurance, which makes no sense. First and foremost, you already know your clients need life insurance. Second, you already know life insurance is lucrative. Life insurance does not generally pay a renewal, but first year commission is going to be anywhere from 70% to 110% of the first-year premium. Lastly, and the most impactful to your bottom line is this: getting the life insurance on an account extends client retention by over 10 years on average. Nobody leaves once you have their life insurance, unless of course....... they use their life insurance.

From my experience, there are a couple of reasons agents do not ask about life insurance. First, it's out of sight and out of mind. One easy fix is stick a post-it on your computer monitor that says, "ask about a life insurance review on every call." The second reason agents do not ask: it is an uncomfortable subject.

Maybe it is the subject of death? Or maybe it is the questions on the application related to financial income, drug use, etc.? This, however, is how you set yourself apart as an agent. Your agents are not salespeople - they are advisors.

Practice role play exercises with your agents to see where your agents might be uncomfortable asking about life insurance. Asking a female client her weight or asking a friend about their personal income might make an agent uncomfortable but the more you role play the easier it gets. You can certainly require at least a life insurance acknowledgement form on every new account (you can find one at thebiggestleap.com). Getting a signed acknowledgement not only provides you with E & O protection, but also it makes the client think more carefully about deciding to plan for their family after their passing.

The last piece on the importance of having full-time clients and the one that may catch your attention most - E & O. No, E & O is not a railroad company on a game board. As you already know, E & O stands for errors and omissions, and it's what happens if you screw up or a client says you screwed up. If your clients are not full-time, then you do not know what other policies they have. Is that engagement ring insured? Maybe. Perhaps the agent handling the earthquake insured it separately, but do you know for certain? Does the insured have an umbrella policy? Maybe. Perhaps it is with the USAA auto insurance policy that your client has separately outside your agency, but again, do you know for certain? The point is that if you do not handle all the insurance, you cannot tell where all the coverage gaps are. Additionally, if you do not handle all the policies, then there will be a lack of coordination between policies that need to be coordinated (e.g., umbrellas with underlying coverage and homeowners and earthquake policies where limits need to match).

Encourage your team to slow down with each client and ensure your team looks at each client holistically and not as a "single sale." No potential agency buyer is going to value your agency based on total number of clients (unless you only have one big client, which is an entirely different issue). Buyers will value your agency on profit; and the larger the average account size, the larger the profit.

Chapter 9: Know When to Fire a Client

The customer is always right, except when they are not. I want to preface this chapter by saying that usually when a customer is upset, frustrated, or disappointed, it is probably within reason and you need to own it and fix it. On occasion, however, you will encounter certain customers who, if taken on, will lead to more headaches and more exposure than they are worth. Your job is to learn to spot them and to avoid them at all costs.

I am sure you have heard the statistics that angry customers tell far more people about their experience than happy customers. If a customer complains very publicly on social media, it is tough to counteract that. Accordingly, as a rule, take care of your customers.

However, there are some customers that your team needs to fire, and fire quickly. There are three types of specific customers I am referring to:

Alan the Abuser: At first, you thought Alan was just having a bad day. He seemed to respond a little over the top to the ID card that arrived late in the mail. A few weeks later, Alan berated your best account manager with a series of F bombs and screaming, leaving her in tears. Then there was the time Alan literally threatened to fight you over a billing issue. Life is too short to deal with the "Alans" of the world. The first time a client abuses you or your staff, give them a warning that such behavior will not be tolerated. Typically, the warning works well as most folks do not want to see themselves as a jerk. They certainly do not want to get "kicked out" of anything for it, and I am not sure how much street cred you get for being kicked out of an insurance agency. Human evolution tells us that being kicked out of any group is generally bad, and you will probably get eaten by lions if left all by yourself. If Alan the Abuser repeats his behavior again, then you must follow through right away and ask him to find a new agent.

Shady Simon: "Well, does my zip code really make a difference in the price? Which zip code is cheapest?" You know this type well. Simon is as slippery as picking up escargot with chopsticks.

To be able to help a customer and do the field underwriting for your carriers, you need customers who are honest. A lot of customers will hold back on their dog type, how much they drive, and what kind of construction their company does; but when directly asked, they will tell the truth. There are some customers who will outright lie to you about key information. It is your job as the agency owner to train your team to understand when someone is holding back versus being plain dishonest. Your team should always remind customers if a claim is ever wrongfully denied that you will absolutely go to bat for them, but you can't do that if they weren't honest on the application.

In the case of Shady Simon, he is going to lie in most cases because, well, he's a liar. Maybe Simon is a pathological liar. Maybe Simon believes insurance companies are evil and it is okay to lie to them to "stick it to the man." Maybe Simon just hopes you magically will not see his four tickets and three accidents. Maybe he simply lacks character and integrity in most areas of his life. The reasons do not matter. Dealing with Shady Simon will hurt your loss ratio, lose you your credibility with carriers, and make you a "shady" insurance operator by association. Shady Simon would be better served by a certain online lizard.

Litigious Lucy: Somebody is going to pay. It does not matter if Lucy tripped over her own two feet in a parking lot, or if her diamond ring she did not want to pay to insure was lost, but *someone* is going to pay. Lucy loves a good fight and seems to enjoy using our legal system as a weapon to be a bully. Of the three "special" personalities in this chapter, Lucy is the one you need to be most cautious about because Lucy can turn out your lights.

Lucy is typically not super concerned about her coverage. She does not necessarily take the minimum limits, but she does not take the coverages you recommend either. You will notice Lucy probably has claim activity in the past five years, and they are probably a decent size. Even with past claims, you notice Lucy is not particularly interested in talking about being covered properly. She wants you to get it done and make sure she has "full coverage" (please, someone strike those words from the public's vocabulary).

When a claim is not covered, Lucy is going to have her attorney send you a letter. Her claim not being covered is your fault no matter what, and she is not happy about it. You are completely incompetent, and you should have known she bought a Rolls Royce she did not tell you about. Shame on you (so she says)! This is going to be an E & O claim for you. The thing about E & O claims is that it makes very little difference whether you are right or wrong. A claim is a claim - it is now on your E & O loss runs, and it will affect your renewal.

If you get a few of these claims, you can find yourself without E & O insurance. Without that, you lose your appointments, and it is lights out for your agency no matter how great your business plan is. Any sort of risk that threatens your agency's very existence must get your attention in a big way, which is why Lucy is so dangerous. Any sort of form you can get signed, or procedure you can follow, that helps you avoid E & O claims is paramount but only half the battle. Avoiding those customers altogether is the other half of the equation. The goal is to prevent claims before they start because once a claim is filed, there is no guarantee what can happen, even when you are completely in the right.

If a case ends up going to a jury trial, please keep in mind juries generally do not like insurance companies. The jury does not differentiate between agencies and carriers so you might as well be Warren Buffet to them. For free forms and procedures to keep you out of a courtroom, go to thebiggestleap.com.

I do want to warn you that you will probably get sued and have to file an E & O claim no matter whether you and your people follow every protocol, have the customer sign every form, and dot every "I." Do not beat yourself up about it, and do not take the suit personally. Just learn from the situation, and move on.

Remember birds of a feather. Any one of the three problem clients we just discussed will refer you friends just like them. Lucky you! The more you can avoid and disassociate from these types of clients, the less likely you are to bring on new ones like them. You will still have Alans, Simons and Lucys who end up in your files; but when you see this character walk in, remember that the best day to lose that deal is day one.

Chapter 10: Specialization

There are riches in niches. If I built an agency over again, the first thing I would do is to specialize in a few focused niche areas. There are several concrete and common-sense reasons to only focus on niches. You already have lots of examples in your own life of niche-focused professionals making more than generalists. An eye surgeon makes more than a general family doctor; a mergers and acquisitions attorney makes more than a general business law attorney; a CPA focusing only on IPOs will make far more than a general practice CPA...you get the picture.

There are several reasons that focusing on niches make sense. The first reason is efficiency. Focusing on niches gives you efficiency gains as an agency, primarily in policy servicing. In a traditional non-niche focused agency (what you might call a "generalist"), the office must deal with several carriers, product types, states, etc. In this generalist environment, account managers must know the logins and contact information for several different insurance carriers. Every time an account manager has to make a policy change with a carrier they are less familiar with, it takes time to figure out the carrier login, figure out the system, and make the actual change. If there is a question for an underwriter, it takes time to figure out who the underwriter is. Dealing with fewer carriers as a specialist agency allows your team to streamline policy changes, commission accounting, mail sorting, etc. A smaller number of carriers also means fewer carrier reps coming into your office to soak up your and your team's time. Your team will also have fewer coverage and systems questions that take up the time of their managers and, ultimately, you. These efficiency gains equal less staff needed to service the business and, therefore, a higher profit margin for your agency, fewer mistakes, and a less stressful environment for your staff.

The second benefit of being niche focused is leverage with your carriers. As you grow your expertise and book size with a particular niche, you can start having conversations with those carriers about marketing support dollars, training resources for your team, and a higher commission schedule for hitting certain goals. It is important to pick a niche that will have a relatively low loss ratio because a niche with a high loss ratio will only cause you headaches.

The goal with the insurance carriers focused on your niche is creating a special, exclusive program solely for your agency; that is the holy grail for any niche focused shop. Having a special program for just your agency with special pricing for your niche creates a figurative moat around your agency; and that makes it very hard to compete with, or take business from, your agency. Having a program creates a "flywheel" within your agency that perpetuates success. Your special program is ideally a specialty with a low loss ratio making your carrier partner happy, allowing them to charge your customers less while paying you enhanced commission. This allows you to attract more customers in this niche while continuing to invest into your business with the additional revenue. Even if your partner insurance carrier decides to leave the business one day, you can always find another carrier partner as long your niche has a low loss ratio and is profitable business.

In addition to efficiency and carrier leverage, a niche-focused agency will also benefit in the areas of advertising and marketing. At the end of the day, most industries are small regarding who the major players are, including the influencers and decision makers. Take our industry - I bet you know most of the agencies within twenty miles of you and can probably name the owners. Whether it is an agency, brokerage, or carrier, gossip travels quickly; and the same people seem to circulate through the business over the years. The same is true with any industry, and it is a huge advantage to any specialty service provider. Your customers will meet at the same industry events, deal with the same vendors, shop at the same suppliers, etc. Once you start to gain traction as an expert in their field with amazing pricing, you will not need to spend a nickel on advertising. If you choose to spend money on advertising (and don't get me wrong, you should!), your money is far better spent focusing on a specific, targeted customer who is far more likely to respond to your advertising because they already know you as an expert in that field.

Once you have established yourself in a niche, get into another one. Having one single niche all by itself is a bad idea. Being an insurance expert solely for mortgage brokers in 2008 would have been very painful. I have watched agencies that specialize in areas like contractors and car dealerships go broke when recessions hit. Once you have success with a particular niche, it is time to start a second, completely unrelated one in a separate industry. It is best to use a totally separate branding strategy so as not to dilute your value as an "expert" in the first niche. You can repeat this strategy as many times as you have the bandwidth for.

If this is such a no brainer, then why don't most agents do it? Honestly, it is difficult to have the discipline to get it started. If you decide to become an expert in insurance for pool contractors as an example, the hard part is not the prospecting of pool contractors or even writing a pool contractor when you find one. <u>The hard part is saying "no" to the restaurant owner who calls you that same day for insurance that she really needs, and you must say no because she is not a pool contractor.</u>

It is never easy to say "no" to business knocking on your door. To be successful as a niche specialist, however, you must be 100% dedicated to saying no to those customers not in your chosen niche. This will absolutely reduce your income in the short term of a year or two. The tradeoff is a practice that is far more profitable than being a generalist long term. Every non-niche client you say "no" to is a step towards building your firm as a specialist.

Even for agencies that focus on personal lines, specialties absolutely exist. Maybe you focus on only doing the personal insurance for professionals like CPAs, attorneys, etc. Maybe you only insure teachers. Maybe you only insure left-handed people (just kidding, but did you know the majority of U.S. Presidents were left-handed?). My point is specialization does not need to be limited to commercial lines. Agencies that specialize in personal lines or even in life and health can specialize and enjoy all the same benefits.

For some ideas on specialization and how to select the right niche for you, check out thebiggestleap.com.

Chapter 11: Direct Appointments, Carrier Access, and Coverage Standards

Carrier access and coverage standards go hand-in-hand. Obviously you want the best carrier contracts possible; but you can only ask for that if you have a great loss ratio, and a great loss ratio comes from coverage standards.

Your goal as an agency owner is to make sure all your carrier appointments are direct. Every time you use a wholesaler or aggregator to place a piece of business, a little genie should jump onto your shoulder and shake you ever so slightly to remind you to stop doing that. When you first start out, you will have to use wholesalers and aggregators to get access to carriers. However, you should always be looking to get that direct appointment and stop using those wholesalers and aggregators as soon as possible. The idea is for all your business to be written on a direct appointment basis. To get direct appointments, you need decent volume and a good loss ratio. In this chapter, we will talk about both of these items and why direct appointments with insurance carriers are so important.

When you first open your doors for business, you will find out quickly that getting an appointment with an insurance carrier is not like getting an appointment with your barber. As a new agency, most carriers will not appoint you unless you can show proof of writing good, clean business for some period of time (usually about three years) along with solid proof that you can write a significant volume of business. This begs the question: If you need to show proof of writing good business with a good carrier for three years, how do you get your first appointment in your first year? It seems like a catch 22, and it is, sort of. With the right strategy, however, you will be able to secure at least a couple of good quality appointments as the first building blocks of your agency.

The first step to getting direct appointments is to know which carriers you even want to do business with. Most agencies, even small agencies, deal with too many carriers and not the carriers that really matter. For example, there are some carriers that will give literally anyone with a license and a pulse an appointment. Those carriers have little value because every agent in town has that appointment. The first question you need to ask yourself is which carriers do you really need to be successful based on your ideal client or niche. If you do not already know the answer to this question, then you need to do some secret shopping with as many agencies as possible to see which carrier or carriers pop up as being truly competitive. Once you identify the list of carriers that you need, it is time to find out who at that carrier controls the appointment process for new agents.

This is another area where relationships are super important. It is not the "company" who is going to decide whether or not to appoint you; it's a real person. That person may be a marketing rep or a VP in charge of overall sales, but somewhere within that carrier it is most definitely a person. I got my most important appointment direct on day one because I had built a meaningful relationship with the carrier's marketing reps and underwriting team while I worked for an agency. This then allowed the marketing rep who made the appointment decision to say "yes" when it would have been easier to say no. If you work for an agency now, start getting to know the reps as best as you can; and make sure they know you are a competent and honest agent.

The second step to getting direct appointments is to have a history of low loss ratio and solid production. Any good carrier will also want to see a solid business plan and solid coverage standards in your business plan. If you are already open for business and do not already know the person you need to speak to at the carrier that you need, then it is back to sales 101 for you to create that relationship. Find out who you need to impress and get busy! Find out what an ideal agency is for that carrier and work hard to become that ideal agency.

So why the big push for direct appointments when a lot of carriers can be accessed via a wholesaler or a cluster? Wholesalers serve a purpose in our business when it comes to certain types of coverage like professional liability, hard-to-place property coverage, high risk business, etc. In some cases, wholesalers have product specific knowledge that has great value. However, on more "vanilla" type policies like auto, home, etc., you want to avoid wholesalers whenever possible for a few key reasons.

First, your commission on any policy through a wholesaler is usually reduced by 1/3. For example, a carrier might pay a 15% commission, but the wholesaler will only pay you 10%. Second, most business through a wholesaler will be agency bill, meaning it is on you to collect the premium, keep your commission, and send the rest to the wholesaler or carrier.

Agency bill policies greatly increase your servicing cost and the risk of having an E & O claim. As you grow, agency accounting can become relatively complicated with a big part of that complication coming from agency bill policies. On top of all of that, wholesalers slow down communication with carriers. In fact, in most cases, you will not be able to talk directly to the carrier you place the business with. Communication then becomes a game of "telephone," and you remember how that game worked as a kid, right? "Ask mom to make me a salami sandwich" becomes "Mom kissed Uncle Charlie don't tell Dad." You cannot risk those types of miscommunications with your clients!

Another option outside of utilizing wholesalers when you can't get a direct appointment can be using a cluster (also known as an "aggregator"). A cluster is an entity that exists solely to give you access to carriers. Over the last several years, a huge number of clusters have popped up so there are many options for a new agency. It is important to be extremely cautious in doing business with a cluster. Joining the wrong cluster can make your agency tougher to sell down the road or can limit your options in other ways. Before you join a cluster, make sure you do your research.

Here are the most important questions you need to ask any aggregator or cluster before going into business with them. In fact, these questions are some important l call them the seven aggregator commandments:

Commandment 1: Thou shalt not give up ownership.

The question you must ask any aggregator is: who owns the business, and how does it work if I want to leave? You must own 100% of the business and be able to leave or sell the business however you see fit. If you do decide to leave the cluster or sell your agency, ensure the cluster does not get any kind of "first right of refusal" to buy your agency or the book you have through that cluster. Do not give up this control under any circumstances. This is crucial.

Commandment 2: Thou shalt get paid by the carrier, not the aggregator.

You always want the carrier paying you directly via direct deposit. In the beginning, you may need to build some volume first to get your own carrier "subcode." A "subcode" is a "child" code to the cluster's "parent" code with the carrier that will typically allow you to get paid directly, among other benefits. Allowing your aggregator to get paid first will delay cash flow and will almost certainly result in some commissions not making their way to you.

Commandment 3: Thou shall talk directly to underwriters.

Good luck explaining a risk to a random account manager at your aggregator so they can explain it to the carrier. The game of telephone usually does not work out so well. Ensure you control your conversations.

Commandment 4: Ensure you can gain your freedom to access carriers on your own someday.

When and how are you able to pursue your own appointments? You do not want to be with a cluster forever so it is important to know this upfront.

Commandment 5: Thou shalt not give up profit sharing bonuses.

Profit sharing from carriers is key to your profitability. It may be reasonable for the cluster to keep some piece depending on whether the cluster charges any other fees to you, but some part of the profit sharing should be shared with you as long as your loss ratio and growth qualifies.

Commandment 6: Thou shalt ask around.

Talk to other agencies that belong to any cluster you are looking at. This is like a job interview. Get references, and find out the things that frustrate existing members.

Commandment 7: Thou shalt get a list in writing of carriers you can access.

Make sure the cluster has all the insurance carriers you need. Dealing with more than one cluster could create a headache so try to find the one with the markets you need.

Not to "beat a dead horse" (who came up with that phrase? Is that something people did often back in the day??), but direct appointments are the goal. They are the only way you can avoid all of the pitfalls of wholesalers and clusters/aggregators we just discussed. When you are fortunate enough to get that direct appointment that you want, treat it seriously and as the privilege that it is. Any new carrier appointment will give you a production requirement, underwriting rules, etc.; and it is important to over-deliver on those items. Delivering on those promises is so important that it is actually better to turn down an appointment if you doubt you can hit the production requirement. It is better to wait on an appointment than to lose an appointment due to lack of production because it can be exceedingly difficult to get those appointments back.

Once you have your appointment, you will likely be assigned a carrier marketing rep. When you find yourself in the position of having several carrier appointments, you also may find yourself overwhelmed with marketing rep meetings. Do not make the mistake of seeing these meetings as a "pain" or an "obligation." Take the carrier rep out to lunch occasionally and even pay the bill! Most agents will never reach for the bill when having lunch with a carrier rep. Be the exception. They are your best source of talented referrals for your team. Marketing reps know all the best account managers, producers and agencies that might one day sell to you, so keep those relationships tight.

In any new carrier relationship, you should of course push for the best commission possible; but you are going to need volume and a good loss ratio to make that happen, so be patient. As far as the "legalese" of a carrier contract, it probably says they have all the control and you essentially have none. Unfortunately, that is just the way it is.

Again, when it comes to these carrier appointments - less is more. Remember that you must feed your carriers, and the last thing you want is to lose an appointment based on lack of production. Only take an appointment when you are confident you can over-deliver to the carrier.

Your chances of getting the very best direct appointments and potentially enormous profit-sharing checks are going to be shaped by your agency coverage standards. Now would probably be a pretty good time to explain exactly what coverage standards are and their purpose.

Coverage standards are there to provide consistency within your book. My own book of business was experiencing high loss ratios with one of my largest carriers, and my marketing rep for that carrier at the time gave me a great lesson on what it means to have coverage standards or in my case, lack thereof. The marketing rep was holding a spreadsheet of 25 random personal auto policies containing data like annual miles, each coverage broken down, status on whether it was a package account, driving history, etc. The spreadsheet showed incredible inconsistency. Since this was a random sample of policies that were written by a variety of my producers, the data varied widely. Some policies had lower annual mileage than others for the same type of commute. Some had medical expense coverage whereas some did not. Some had rental car reimbursement whereas some did not. Some had homeowners' insurance attached whereas some did not. You get the idea. If Forrest Gump had seen this list, he would have thought it was more random than a box of chocolates.

My marketing rep explained, "Tim, you have absolutely no consistency here, and it is driving your high loss ratios." I was surprised because I thought I <u>did</u> have coverage standards. The producers at my agency knew any homeowners should have limits of 250/500 on their auto insurance at a minimum, not to take on insureds with a certain number of claims, the need for accurate mileage, and so on. The rules I had created were a good starting point, but clearly not enough.

Agency coverage standards should, and do, vary from one agency to another. There are, however, a few areas that make sense for any agency owner. Below is a list of the things that should be your standards if you want to keep a low loss ratio (and your sanity):

• Higher deductibles. Create a minimum deductible in your office. Claims frequency hurts your client and your agency so keep the deductibles high.

• Create standards on which coverages are always included. Should your home policies always include extra sewer backup coverage? Should your business package policies with a certain carrier always include data breach? Should your auto insurance policies always include rental car reimbursement? Those questions are up to you, but the answer should be consistent across all policies.

• Rewrites for nonpayment. In a word: Stop. Rewriting customers who continue to cancel for nonpayment will drive your loss ratios through the roof and your employees insane. There is always the situation where a great customer let their policy cancel due to an unusual circumstance, but that needs to be the exception. Remember that every time a client and/or your producer explains why the policy lapsed, it will sound like a one-time "unlikely to every happen again" (the insured was rescuing puppies in another country and missed the payment date by one day) event. Don't do it.

Special side note regarding my strong feelings against rewriting policies for nonpayment. A lot of it has to do with rating regulations specific to being in California. California does not allow consideration of credit rating on personal auto policies, which means a premium for someone with a 500-credit score will be the same as someone with an 800-credit score. In other states that use credit scoring, customers with a poor payment history will pay more; and the higher premium might make up for the inconvenience that rewriting the policy creates. *Maybe.*

If you follow some of the tactics in this chapter, you will end up with a low loss ratio and great carriers that you can feed business to often. This is a recipe for a very profitable agency. This assumes, of course, that the carriers you work with have some sort of profit-sharing plan you can qualify for. If they do not, you should reconsider whether they are a good agency partner.

The only reason you should work with a carrier that does not pay profit sharing is if they pay an unusually large percentage of commission up front and at renewal. I have seen agents work with carriers that have no profit-sharing opportunity and pay substandard renewal commissions. That is unacceptable. We have tremendous value as agents; and it is critical that as an insurance agency owner, insurance agent, and part of the larger agent community, you stand up and advocate for yourself and our profession. <u>There is no carrier so critical to have that it is worth settling for less than you deserve.</u> You get what you tolerate in life. Do not tolerate any carrier taking you "for a ride" on agency compensation.

There are, of course, a couple assumptions to the rousing speech I just made (I felt like Russell Crowe speaking to an arena full of insurance agents). You must have low loss ratios and solid production to have the leverage to demand anything. Otherwise you will be stuck taking whatever contract you are given. It can take a few years before you can bring this subject up with carrier marketing reps, but always have it on your mind.

Paying attention to where you place business and implementing your own coverage standards will put you ahead of probably 90% of other agents. Doing this correctly will require saying no to certain insurance companies and certain clients now for more opportunity and better results in the future. Anytime you have the option to delay gratification, do it!

Chapter 12: Consolidate Your Business with Fewer Carriers

Did you know McDonald's used to sell ribs, mashed potatoes, turkey sandwiches, pot roast and about fifty other items they do not offer today? That's right! The McDonald brothers' original restaurant sold a variety of menu items at their original carhop location. The restaurant did good business but was terribly inefficient. Just think about having to keep ingredients on hand for such a large amount of menu items, having to teach your servers the entire menu, show cooks how to cook numerous items, etc.

The McDonald brothers saw an opportunity to be smarter about their business so they closed their restaurants for several months to simplify their operation with a focus on efficiency. They reopened as a walk-up restaurant with only three items: hamburgers, French fries and milkshakes. That's it! The first several customers to visit the newly reopened McDonalds asked for their usual favorites and were dismayed to find the restaurant now only had three items. "You'll be closed in 3 months!," one of the patrons erroneously predicted.

As I am sure you well know, McDonald's not only stayed open, but thrived. The new concept became known throughout the city of San Bernadino as a place to grab a consistent, fast, and delicious hamburger at a great price. The key to being able to give customers a great value and be profitable in the process is efficiency.

"Most companies don't die from starvation; they die from indigestion."

That's a quote from Dave Packard of Hewlett Packard, and it is a quote I tend to agree with. That first McDonald's restaurant with over fifty menu items is what I see when I walk into most insurance agencies.

A lot of agencies pride themselves on running a boat insurance quote with eight insurance carriers or shopping a small business package policy with eleven carriers over a span of five hours for a $75 commission. I would say I am exaggerating a bit; but with many agencies, this is the reality! It makes no sense! Your job is to narrow down your client's needs and situation to locate the right carrier with a good policy at a fair price. It is not to drown your client with a fire hose of every quote from every insurer who serves that market. What makes us invaluable to the client compared to an automated online insurance tool is for us to find the best coverage for their needs, not just the best price.

Most customers who say the price is most important do not really mean it for two reasons. First, most customers know very little about insurance. One thing that they do understand is what the insurance will cost. Second, focusing on price is a defense mechanism. It's the customer saying "hey, I'm paying attention so don't screw me!" Nobody wants to be taken advantage of. The client's stated focus on price is why so many agents think they need to quote a renters policy with a dozen carriers; but in the end, it is simply not true. Show the client you care, that you are competent, and that you have their best interests and their needs at heart, and most will go with you.

One of the keys to efficiency in an insurance agency is carrier consolidation. Why is this so important, and how does it benefit you and your agency?

Imagine the average account manager's day for a moment. A client calls in to make a change to their 1) boat insurance with Progressive, 2) motorcycle policy with Nationwide, and 3) home insurance with Safeco. The next call is 4) a client with a home and auto package through a regional carrier, 5) followed by an email from someone who just had a claim with Kemper. This all happens within half an hour. Within those thirty minutes, the account manager must log into five carriers' sites and navigate five different systems.

Assuming these carriers are used often, perhaps the passwords are saved. If the carriers are used less frequently, then the account manager will be searching for passwords. Add to that, many carriers are now adding multi-factor authentication to their logins or frequently changing login credentials. There are not only passwords to manage, but also carrier specific endorsements to remember, different systems to navigate, carrier downloads to manage, etc. Every carrier you do business with has a cost to your agency and it is significant. Less is more.

Recognize which products in your agency truly require marketing with multiple carriers. For one-off policies like watercraft, personal article floaters, certain types of business policies, and the like, try to stick to one single carrier. Use the same thinking with wholesalers. Try to narrow down the number of wholesalers you work with to no more than three. If you find that you "need" more than three wholesalers because your book of business requires it, then that might be a sign that your book is too spread out and not focused enough on a particular type of client or business. As we discussed, it is far better for your firm to be a more focused niche player, or at the very least, have a target client.

A final reason for putting your business with fewer carriers is that it could help you avoid a catastrophic E & O claim. I know I have already talked about E & O claims, but I want to stress: do not have E & O claims.

Given the fact that an E & O claim could put you out of business and bankrupt you at the same time, I think this is the type of subject that bears a little repeating. The reality is that the world is becoming more litigious every day, and the size of judgments are increasing annually. If the claim goes to the jury, the bias against you as an extension of an insurance company that is universally hated will be strong. The reality is that your agency *will* get hit with some E & O claims - it is unfortunately just part of business. With the tips in this book, I hope that they are just a nuisance and not a catastrophe.

Similar to using wholesalers as we discussed earlier, dealing with multiple carriers increases the likelihood of E & O claims significantly. Remember that account manager dealing with five carriers in less than 30 minutes? Do you think the account manager might be more likely to make an error in a scenario with the complexity of five carriers or a situation with one or two carriers? Complexity increases the chance of errors in any situation. Add to that the fact that every carrier has their own endorsements, exclusions, and policy forms with unique questions. As an example, we had a carrier partner that covered our personal lines customers with dwelling fire policies. One day, the carrier decided to remove personal injury coverage from every renewal as the policies renewed. There was no announcement or special cover letter on the policies - the coverage was just deleted as each policy renewed. Thankfully an astute account manager who worked closely with this carrier noticed the difference on a declaration page and informed our team, and we were able to begin moving business away from this carrier the very next day.

The goal is for your team to know everything about the carrier better than any other agent out there, and you can only get to that level if you deal with fewer carriers. Fewer carriers will reduce possible errors and will ensure your team members understand what they are selling to the customer.

To be clear, I am saying to work with fewer carriers, but not only one carrier (or two or three). I know an independent agency that deals with literally just one carrier. This agency is, in a lot of ways, the poster child for this chapter. The agency is simple, efficient, and wildly profitable. However, if that one carrier changes their business appetite or if somehow that agency loses their appointment, it is lights out for that agency. Have your eggs in fewer, but not just one, basket.

Chapter 13: Understanding Your Numbers and Data

As an agency gets off the ground, the agency owner typically accounts for at least a good portion, if not all, of new business production. In time, with a lot of hard work and a little bit of luck, the agency hires a few producers and gains some traction in the community. The agency hums along and is killing it in the new business category. The agency owner is having his/her best year ever in personal production, the producers are exceeding their new business goals, and the couple of account managers who were hired are also writing business too! Revenue is up significantly each quarter, new prospects are pouring in, the profit looks fantastic, and the bank account is...empty. Empty!? Wait, what!? How can you run out of cash if you are profitable?

There are three documents that tell you the true financial health of your agency. The first is your *profit & loss statement.* This tells you if your business is operating at a profit or loss and what the bottom-line number is. Regardless of how you "feel" the business is doing, this is the final report card as to how well you are running your business. Hint: you need the final profit number to be positive.

What should your profit be? Good question! A really well-run agency might have a margin of 30% whereas yours might be closer to 10%. Do not get down on yourself if your final number is not huge! Those family dinners, car payments, cell phone allowance for your kids, and "business" trips to Hawaii would be counted as profit if you ever were to sell. Obviously, do not go overboard on the write-offs as that would be starving your business of the money it needs to grow. Generally speaking, your agency's profitability taking into account those "owner's perks" should not be less than 20%. We will talk in Chapter 14 about why that 20% number is important.

Another key factor that affects profitability includes how much of the business you write versus other producers. If you are a producer, you want to get to a point where you pay yourself the same as every other producer so you can get a true sense of profitability.

The second financial document that matters is your *balance sheet*. A balance sheet is simply a financial screenshot of a moment in time, showing your assets and liabilities at that time. I like thinking of your "cash" balance like the oil in your car: if it gets low, your business will come to a halt. By the way, I am not referring to the cash in your "trust" account, as using those dollars for yourself wins you a free pair of silver bracelets and a trip to Club Fed. A balance sheet shows where you are at. It is the result of how you have been running your business, but probably will not give you amazing operational data.

The final financial document that does not get mentioned nearly as often as the first two is your *cash flow statement*. When it comes to making sure your business is operating in a way that allows you to pay your bills and take money home, <u>this</u> is the one to watch like a hawk. The number you want to look for is "net cash from operations." That is the number you have left over at the end of each week, month, or year, depending on how you ran the report.

You might feel like you are doing amazingly well, not realizing that you are sucking up cash every month. If you are growing fast, you will notice your cash gets squeezed as you need to pay new hires, rent more space, buy more software licenses, etc. Keep a careful eye on that net cash from operations number, and make sure it does not start heading in the wrong direction.

Strong growth and low cash may be an indicator that you need to take a loan to finance your growth. If your profit & loss statements show your growing operation is profitable, that might not be a bad idea.

One last bit of advice before we move on from financial documents. I am going to go out on a limb and say that you might not love financial documents. You might be thinking, "yeah I know it's important, but I have my CPA for that." Even if your CPA is the most trustworthy and competent CPA in your town, you must understand your numbers as the business owner. You must understand exactly how your business is doing financially before you make a new hire, acquire an agency, buy a building, or sell your agency. This is not knowledge that you can delegate to someone else. You must understand your financials.

By the way, one bonus of understanding your financials is the ability to more effectively analyze the financials of agencies that you might buy. If you understand a seller's financials better than they do, that puts you in a position to see value that they might not see.

As you can see, growing a successful agency is about a lot more than just strong sales. Strong sales are like water: it is a must have to grow your firm, but too much can be a real problem. It is said that strong sales can solve any issue, but that is not really a true statement. A more accurate statement is "strong sales can delay or mask almost any problem." There are a variety of important metrics to pay attention to. New business sales is just one of those metrics, albeit a very important one.

Once you understand the financial piece, you can zone in on operations. How many customers and/or policies should your account managers handle? How many account managers should you have based on the size of your firm? How do you know your producers are really excelling compared to other firms? Just because your account managers and producers are incredibly busy does not mean you are doing well as an agency. Knowing the data on your agency's operations and how they compare to other agencies is also key.

A great resource I recommend for knowing what your agency should look like is the book *Growth & Performance Standards* from the National Alliance for Insurance Education and

Research. This is a great book detailing several key performance indicators (KPIs) based on your geographic area, agency size, etc.

Our agency has a KPI spreadsheet we update monthly to see exactly where we are compared to goals. You can view this spreadsheet and download a version for yourself at thebiggestleap.com. Always look at your KPIs and financials before making any decision on a future commitment like a lease, a new hire, or other decision that is not easily reversible. Just like I mentioned with your financials, KPIs will also show how you are *really* doing compared to how you *feel* you are doing. Numbers do not lie. They will tell you the real story every time.

Being able to steer your agency in the right direction assumes you know where you are. If you want to be able to manage your agency based on accurate data, you need to have a good place to pull that data from; and that is where your agency management system comes into play. There are several agency management systems in the marketplace, and it is not one size fits all. When our agency first started and for the first ten years, we used an agency management geared more towards personal lines; and we did our accounting in QuickBooks. Once we got to a point of more complexity, we moved to a more robust agency management system and moved our accounting into that system. That move was *really* hard on everyone in the agency. Sometimes a move is unavoidable, but learn from my experience and go with the most robust agency management system you can from day one. More importantly, make sure you and your team know how to use it.

An agency management system is about far more than storing customer data. Utilize your agency management system for everything you can based on what type of business you focus on. Here are a few quick tips from the 10,000-foot level:

- Use downloads. If your carriers offer downloads, be sure to use them and correct them as they come in.
- Fill in every field on every account the day you set it up. Fields like premium, commission, NAICs (for commercial), contacts, etc. are useful. Get the fields filled in from day one when you setup the client.
- Ensure every policy document, client communication, note, etc. goes into your agency management files.

- Invest in training. Train your team members when you get the system, when you hire someone new, and then continue training every month for everyone, including you.
- Join a community for your agency management system. Most companies will have a user community group you can join to learn more and learn the best practices.
- Use the reporting feature. Understand which reports are useful to you, and run them often.
- Lastly, police the accuracy of your data religiously. It is "garbage in, garbage out" so <u>do not allow any inaccurate information</u> to live in your system. Ensure your entire team understands this. The benefits to understanding your data are endless.

Being able to make sense of your data and numbers will not only provide significant dividends to your operations, but also you will be able to get to your final goal far more accurately and quickly. As mentioned, if you are doing any kind of acquisitions, this skill is non-negotiable. Most agency owners unfortunately do not understand their numbers or KPIs. Worse yet, they are probably tracking neither.

Chapter 14: Producer Contracts and How Much to Pay Producers

The single most common question I see agency owners ask each other is "how much do you pay your producers?" That kind of question is like a customer asking you what an insurance policy costs without telling you to what kind of policy they are referring.

Producer commissions and the producer contracts used with producers vary greatly from agency to agency. This is an area you will want to pin down before hiring producers because it is very difficult to change producer commission split agreements once established. If you already have producers, you might find out that you are paying too much or that you have a bad contract with them (or maybe no contract with them). Regardless of the boat you are in, this is an area you want to take seriously from the start as it will ultimately determine your agency's profitability and value if you sell.

So, how much *should* you pay your producers? It depends.

The first big question is "who services the

business?" One very common setup for agencies is where account managers do the servicing work, while producers focus on sales. What about items that might not fall under "servicing" like quoting, claim follow up, remarketing, etc. As is usually the case, the devil is in the details.

Generally, smaller agencies will have producers doing more work out of necessity. A small agency is not going to have legal counsel and claims specialists. Another question is whether your producers are W2 vs 1099. Be extremely careful about having producers as 1099. Be sure to check with more than one CPA and an employment attorney or, at a minimum, someone very familiar with insurance agencies such as your local agent association. Regulations over whether your producers can be 1099 versus W2 vary state-by-state. If you misclassify your folks, that can be an agency-ending mistake, if the penalties are large enough.

Assuming for a moment that your agents are W2, that you service their business, and that they generally do not pay for their office space, computer, phone, etc., then a fair producer split is going to be around 40% new and 35% renewal to the producer. That is a general rule meant to give you a starting point. You may want to pay a higher new business commission to bigger producers as the new business commission rate will not affect your profitability nearly as much as what you give away at renewal. On some product types like life insurance, you can afford to pay more because the servicing cost is next to nothing; but stay firm on that 40/35 number for most products. The biggest single reason a multi-person insurance agency will lack profitability is due to paying producers too high of a split.

When I started my agency in 2008, I paid 50/50 on new and renewal to my producers. Learn from my mistake, and do not do that. I thought it would attract quality salespeople, which it did; but the reality shifted to being unable to afford to hire quality service staff, run a quality operation with the right software, pay for dependable technology, attract quality clients, etc., all while making a profit. The math just does not work, and I found out within the first year that I was not going to make a dollar of profit as long as I was paying 50/50.

If you ask producers what they think is fair, you might get a number like 90% or maybe 100% and the shirt off your back. Most producers will feel they are underpaid, and it makes sense - they have no idea what is involved in running an agency. I was always very transparent about our agency's financial performance with our team because I wanted producers to understand that their deal was actually a fair one and that if they decided to go out on their own, they would ultimately make less money and have more headaches.

Your goal as an agency owner is to keep your final profit margin at 20% or more of your gross revenue, and that is before any carrier contingency bonuses because those are not guaranteed. You can certainly operate with a lower margin, especially if you are collecting separate commissions as a producer writing business; but there are a few significant challenges with having a margin under 20%.

First, if your margin is under 20% and a soft market hits, your revenue might fall faster than you can realistically cut expenses. You could find yourself in the red pretty quickly.

Second, if you are funding your growth with cash flow, it will be difficult to grow the business and feed your family with a tight profit margin. You will end up funding one of the two with debt, which is never a good idea. Remember that cash flow statement we talked about in the last chapter? The cash you generate from operations must be positive.

Lastly, the expenses showing in your profit and loss statement are far from your only expenses. You have a couple other massive expenses you must take into account: your risk and your time.

If something goes sideways and a massive E & O claim occurs, your producers and staff members can always get another job. However, you as the owner do not have that luxury to walk away. Any significant lawsuit or demand not covered by your own insurance or exceeding your insurance falls on you whether that is fair or not. There is a cost to having that kind of risk, and your margin should compensate for that.

Also, from a time standpoint, running an agency sucks up a lot of that. Eventually you will get to a point where you can delegate more and enjoy more freedom, but you do not have that freedom in your first few years. Your time spent building your agency is time away from your home, your family, your friends, your hobbies, etc.; and there is a cost for that. Pay yourself what you are worth, and watch that end profit number like a hawk.

Remember: revenue is vanity, profit is sanity, and cash is king. Do not overpay producers.

Alright, so you have a fair producer split and now you need to memorialize it somewhere. There is always the idea of documenting the split via a neck tattoo on the producer, but that might make it hard for that producer to sell new policies (or not difficult, depending on your clientele). It is probably a better idea to have a contract. **Always** have a contract. Employing your son? Have a contract. Employing your dad? Have a contract. Employing your pastor? Have a contract. A contract serves not only to protect you in the event of a disagreement but also to provide clarity when conversations eventually get forgotten or remembered differently.

To help get you started, I have included a contract template at thebiggestleap.com. Before using it, please review this contract with your attorney to ensure that you understand it and to confirm you are complying with local and state laws.

This contract might seem long at thirty-three pages, but that is pretty simple by today's standards. My first contract with my producers was a single page, and I would have preferred to keep it that way; but the reality is there are many items that must be covered in a contract, in addition to producer splits. In addition to any changes your attorney tells you to make, make the changes that matter to you and your producers. Just make sure that you own the business or at least have "first right of refusal." Otherwise, your insurance agency is not sellable, as I will explain.

Before starting my own agency, I worked for that other small property & casualty agency I previously mentioned as a producer for four years. My contract at that agency gave me equity in my book of business that I earned over time and allowed me to buy out my entire book at a predetermined price if I ever wanted to leave. This contract was the same contract that my then boss had had with his boss twenty years prior and which had allowed him to open his own agency. This same contract might have gone back to the building of the pyramids for all I know, and I was certainly ready to perpetuate the contract with my producers and I did just that. I did not know better and just figured that is the way producer contracts work! Producers always have the right to buy their book if they want to do so at a certain point, but the reality is that that is not the way it usually works.

I am not against allowing producers to have equity in their book. I actually think that it makes a lot of sense and can be crucial to recruiting and retaining the right kind of producers. Producers work hard to build their book; and, in most agencies, the producers are doing their own prospecting so the relationships are theirs anyways. In my experience, folks with ownership in an organization will work harder, be more loyal, and think like an owner instead of like an employee.

I think some agency owners hear the idea of giving their producers book ownership and worry that that makes any producer more likely to leave, but I believe it actually has the opposite effect. Giving a producer book ownership can be pretty smart. The important thing is which party has the first right of refusal to purchase the book if your producer does leave or you decide to sell.

On the subject of "right of first refusal," my advice is easy: you, as the agency owner, must have first right of refusal on the producer's book of business. Period. Without a right of first refusal on all of the business in the agency, you are not able to sell the agency because the producers can just buy you out and leave before the sale. You would then be left with no producers and nothing to sell, which is the last place you want to be. A right of first refusal just means if either you or the producer decide they want a change to the status quo, that it is your right to have first dibs on the book.

Why would a producer sign a contract that gives you first right of refusal? Well, for one, let's hope that they can trust you. In reality, this should not be a concern. If the producer wants to leave one day to start their own firm, the right of first refusal would mean they would have to ask you to buy their book, but there would not really be any point to trying to stop them. Sure, just like my old boss, you can try to talk them out of it by bringing them a case or even a pallet of their favorite beer, tickets to the World Series, and the keys to a new car; but by the time a producer tells you they are leaving, it is over.

By the time a producer tells you that they are leaving, they have been thinking about it for quite some time and probably rehearsed their "Jerry Maguire" speech several times in their head. If you do successfully get a producer to change his/her mind and stay, there is a pretty good chance the clock on that relationship is ticking. If a producer wants to leave, they will leave. The producer controls the client relationship. If you try to fight that or get into it legally with a producer, you will only benefit the attorneys and will lose the clients anyway.

Your first right of refusal on the book of business is something that will take on greater importance the more that you grow. Banks will want to see the first right of refusal. Investors will want to see the right of first refusal. If you sell, the buyer will <u>need</u> to see right of first refusal.

So now you have the first right of refusal on buying the book, but for how much? Remember that one of the most important reasons to have a contract in place is for clarity for both parties. The value of a book of insurance business can vary quite a bit. When I bought my book of business in 2008, the valuation was at 1.5x times the gross revenue of the book. Right now, that number is closer to 2 to 2.5x for a producer's book. These numbers might be a bit lower than you expected, but remember a producer's book is worth a lower multiple than an agency's book.

An agency has a brand, system, appointments, etc. whereas a producer's book of business is based around a person. Agency valuations as a multiple of top line revenue have gone anywhere from 2x to more than 4x over the past decade. Several agency factors will ultimately affect any valuation, and that valuation will change over time. This brings up another good point about any important contract in life: they need to be updated periodically.

In the case of your producer contracts, you and your producers should re-evaluate the buyout multiple every few years to ensure it is as close to market as possible. Any contract left in a drawer for 20 years and then only reviewed when it is time to use it (like a will, living trust, etc.) is going to have items that are dangerously outdated. As your agency grows and your producers mature and grow their own books, their contracts will change as well so it is best to look at any contract as a living document that changes over time for the benefit of all.

Remember that a good contract is not meant to keep your producers "locked" into a situation that they do not want to be in. A good contract just provides clarity and guidance on what each party's roles are and what happens if you and your producer need to separate. Your producers will be approached every week by other agencies wanting to recruit them, many of which are willing to pay them more... sometimes much more. Keep a close relationship with your producers; help them grow; and whatever you do, never take them for granted and you will keep the good ones.

Chapter 15: Community Involvement

You already know people do business with people they like. It seems like no surprise then that people also buy from companies they like. If you can win someone's heart, you can win their wallet (that sounded far colder than I anticipated!).

The biggest part of my agency's brand is community involvement, and it has paid dividends both personally and professionally that I cannot even begin to explain. The professional benefits come in the form of customer referrals, employee referrals, positive press, and a genuinely positive culture within our company. I would love to tell you the community piece was a brilliant strategic move that I designed specifically to get all of these great benefits, but that is simply not true.

Our community involvement, and my own community involvement, happened by accident. While working as a producer before opening my own firm, I was approached about serving on a small board for the local YMCA. I was 22 years old, and the idea of sitting on a board seemed like a big deal. Did these people call the right "Tim?" Why would they invite me on their board?? It turns out

I was recommended by someone I met at a Chamber of Commerce event, and apparently I looked like a good fit.

I was more flattered than anything else and was worried they would find out who I really was and kick me right off the board. I didn't know much about the YMCA, but I was very familiar with the community they served, having grown up in the neighborhood all my life.

I met with the Executive Director of the organization. He told me about the Y's mission and the wonderful programs they provided to the community and invited me to sit in on a board meeting. I accepted the invitation to attend the meeting as a "fly on the wall" and just watched. I am sure that for all of the existing board members, it was just a pretty typical board meeting. For me, it was something new and exciting. I knew the organization was one I wanted to be a part of, and I was in awe of the people. There were CEOs, local politicians, and other local leaders. My game plan was to shut up, not make a fool of myself, and hope the group voted me in; and they did!

I did not realize at the time how just one board position could impact my life. The thing about being involved in non-profit work and serving on boards is that you are surrounded by kind hearted, giving, eager, like-minded people. The other people you meet on boards are typically successful, positive people who also want to make a difference in their community. I began meeting people who inspired and challenged me as a person, a businessman, and a community member to be better. One board became two boards, and over time the organizations and boards I became involved in became larger and populated with the exact type of people I wanted to meet. I now sit on three boards that I am very passionate about, and the people I have met in these organizations are some of the most talented, philanthropic, and well-known people in Los Angeles. I have had not only amazing business opportunities, but also unparalleled opportunities to grow as a person and elevate my own goals. The secret is that I was never after social mobility or the ability to name drop. I just want to do good and serve, and this is the key to some of the best opportunities for fulfillment in life. It just so happens that those opportunities are not bad for business.

These organizations need support. They need sponsors to financially underwrite the events and programs within the city on a regular basis. It is a natural fit for our company to be a leading sponsor in many of these events, and we do so consistently with the "consistency" piece being the key. If you decide to sponsor a gala or a little league team for a single night, or even a single season, you cannot expect much in return from an ROI standpoint. However, if you are the year-after-year sponsor of that same organization, people will start to remember. They will tie your company to the support you provide that organization. In the eyes of the public, a company that sponsors one event does it for marketing purposes; but a company that supports an organization over many years does so because they care. It is the companies that care that people want to buy from and work for.

Does it matter what organization you are involved in? As long as it is something that speaks to your heart, then it will speak to other folks' hearts as well. You will feel personal fulfillment and enjoyment out of your participation, which is palpable to others. It is important to do something you feel a connection with, or you will lose interest quickly or seem disingenuous. I will say that somewhat larger organizations like a YMCA, Boys and Girls Club, etc. do have some greater benefit because they tend to have more structure and stability.

The idea of giving back is sort of a no-brainer to me. It is a win-win proposition for all involved. I do want to give a word of caution about getting involved in organizations that are divisive or more political in nature. Unless it is by design, aligning yourself or your company with a particular ideology or political agenda is going to alienate a good percentage of customers and potential employees. Once you own a business, you essentially give up the right to let your feelings be known on social media or to put that bumper sticker on your car. Think of you and your business as Switzerland, and be careful not to get drawn into heated topics. You never know what key customer, legislator, vendor, commissioner, carrier, etc. might feel very differently than you do and take offense. Better to have people know your company as the organization that helps fund kids' lunches, heal turtles, or provide swimming lessons.

One final note: people have varying opinions about doing the insurance for the actual group they support. In some cases, the bylaws of a non-profit organization will actually prohibit you from handling the insurance of the non-profit that you support because of a conflict of interest. In my opinion, the best bet is to not solicit the insurance at all because if nothing else, it looks bad.

However, if the organization you support needs your help with the insurance, then make them a client.

Chapter 16: Building Your Team, The Importance of A-Players

I am going to take a wild guess and say that you might be the type of person used to doing it all. I say that because you obviously want to build your own agency - you at least made the investment in this book, and I bet this is not the first book about building an agency that you have purchased. I would assume you want to aggressively build your agency because you are good at a lot of the pieces involved in starting to build an agency. Many agency owners are great at sales, customer service, and marketing. If you are energetic and generally competent, your default will be to do things yourself. However, as you might already suspect or will soon find out, you cannot do everything yourself. The goal in building any organization and being an effective CEO is to put yourself out of a job.

There is a fantastic author, Jim Collins, who wrote the book *Good to Great*, which is a must read for anyone in business. A key idea Jim talks about is the importance of having the right people on the bus and the right people in the right seats. You can have big dreams, processes you want to implement, and grand expansion plans; but without the right people, you cannot do any of it. At the very least, you cannot scale it beyond yourself and the number of hours you can work.

The first and biggest question any entrepreneur has is where to find the people to join your team. Not just any people, but how do you find *A-players*? I hope it is A-players that you are looking for, but perhaps you have read *Moneyball* and you are planning on being the Billy Beane of insurance.

For those of you unfamiliar with the book by Michael Lewis, *Moneyball* and the movie adaptation starring Brad Pitt is the true story of the Oakland A's baseball team and how they recruit less expensive "passed over" talent to build a team that wins, despite having the smallest payroll in Major League Baseball. The team's general manager, Billy Beane (played by Brad Pitt), was focused on only the aggregate number of hits. He did not care about fielding, behavior, attitude, pitching or anything else - just the number of hits. The theory was that hits win games, which turned out to be accurate with the team performing phenomenally well with a tiny budget.

Well, will that work for you, Insurance Billy Beane? What if you just focus on people who can write business no matter their behavior or work in any other area? Is it possible that you can focus solely on people who can produce and things will fall into place because enough sales can solve any problem? I think that would be a very bad idea.

The truth is that enough sales can *mask* any problem. Having big sales is great - it can create the cash flow you need to fund growth. New business sales is one of the key ingredients in building a great agency. As we talked about earlier, however, growing too fast can strip away your cash more quickly than the commissions come in. Another problem is that sometimes a healthy sales volume can actually make you a lazy operator. Are your account managers handling enough files, and is each account manager profitable on their own? Is the marketing you are doing generating adequate ROI? Is your culture healthy, or is there resentment and disengagement happening? If you have healthy sales, it can actually mask some of these issues.

The problem with the Moneyball approach in insurance is that healthy sales do not last forever without a well-run business and a great team as a foundation. Strong sales will grow your number of clients, meaning you will need a strong service infrastructure. A strong service infrastructure will require more account managers, which will require a competent recruiting team and a healthy employee culture.

Having a healthy culture will require employees' needs being attended to and that management is responsive and paying attention. This all goes back to the point of this chapter; you need to have A-players on board. A-players create a strong team, and a strong team can do anything we just talked about without your having to figure it all out yourself.

As Reed Hastings pointed out in his book *No Rules Rules*, hiring only A-players gives you "talent density," which allows you to create *fewer* rules. Think about the different guidelines and rules you have in your office. They might be things like "always return emails and calls the same day" or "be sure to have manager approval before paying some cost for a client." These rules and many more were created because an employee dropped the ball in the past.

Perhaps you have problematic C- and D-players who routinely return emails two or more days later, team members who never seem to get their applications signed, or account managers who do not make policy changes in a timely fashion. These problems are all unacceptable and need to be addressed, right? To combat these problems going forward, you end up creating a rule about returning emails, a rule about signing apps, and a rule about the timeliness of submitting policy changes. These C- and D-players will make many mistakes, forcing you to create many rules. If you have A-players, you can simply trust your team members to make good decisions; and many rules will be unnecessary.

You already know an "A-player" in other industries. It is your favorite waiter at your favorite restaurant who knows who you are and always remembers your order. It is the teller at your bank for whom you wait every time because you know they will handle your transaction quickly and accurately.

In your company, the A-player is the person you end up tasking with everything because they have the capacity, energy, and the will to get things done and get them done correctly. An A-player is not naturally good at everything, but they put 110% of themselves into every project and learn how to make it work. They need to figure out a solution because that is who they are, and their worst fear in life is letting you down.

Compare this person to an "average" team member who clocks in a couple of minutes after the start time, delivers projects on time sometimes but a bit late just as often, and delivers just enough to stay off your radar. The difference in value, output, and company contribution from an A-player is *ten times* that of the average employee. Before we get into finding A-players, let's start with something more important: do not lose the A-players you already have!

Occasionally, you will get lucky and an A-player will land in your lap. The trick is to recognize what you have and make sure that you treat that person like your very best customer. Your job is to serve that A-player, not the other way around. Keep A-players happy, and they will attract more A-players because birds of feather flock together. Do this, and you will not need to worry about having to source A-players from scratch.

Perhaps you have not been lucky yet, or maybe you were a bit too demanding on that A-player who left your company. First, remember people do not leave bad jobs; they leave bad managers. Recognize your part in any A-player's departure because **you are 90% of the reason that person left.** That is a tough thing to accept, but it is true. This is true even though I bet the person had a very good reason to leave, like they were moving to be closer to family, going back to school, or entering a different industry. It is no use recruiting A-players if you ultimately cannot keep them. It is akin to bailing water out of a boat that has a hole in it. There is not enough room in this book to dig into how to be a great leader, but I can tell you that step one is getting honest feedback from your current and past team members, even if it isn't pretty. I have created some resources you can use at thebiggestleap.com to get started on evaluating your own leadership impact.

Now, assuming you are not going to chase off the amazing people you find, where do you find A-players? Well, I will start with where you will find them. You probably will not find A-players with online job ads. Think about who responds to job ads; it is typically someone out of a job who is looking for a job. A-players are never out of a job. Nobody ever fires or lays off an A-player. When a company does layoffs, who gets laid off first? The less competent a team member is, the more expendable they are.

When you place an ad online for a job, the general rule is that you are going to get the bottom of the barrel. The exception to this rule occurs when you have a recession or economic shift that creates massive layoffs in a certain industry. Think mortgage brokers in 2008. In a situation where lots of people are out of a job all at once, some A-players will be looking online for the right job for them.

A-players are already working, but they are probably not being appreciated wherever they are. Remember I mentioned you probably chased away your past A-players? Well, that's so common in business that it is actually the norm.

A-players in most companies are taken for granted and either not valued, not given enough opportunity to shine, not given appropriate acknowledgement, or are so depended upon that they are doing the work of five people without commensurate recognition; and that is good news for you! This gives room for a conversation to be had. You just need to be the one to create the opportunity for a conversation. Here are a few ideas to find A-players and create an opportunity for a conversation.

- Most important and effective idea first: your current employees! Your current team members know great people. They just need a nudge to make an introduction. I suggest a significant recruiting bonus to current team members who recruit new team members. "Significant" means $1500, not $100. This is obviously most effective if your current team includes some A-players.
- Industry events. Do you go to industry events? Perhaps your local insurance agent industry group or other insurance related organization? Those are great places to network for talent. Get to know people on a personal level so they like you, and they will be hoping you bring an employment opportunity.
- Diamonds in the rough. Do you ever go to a coffee shop and wonder, "how does that barista remember all those orders and make those drinks so quickly?" Or perhaps the guy you bought a car from was super knowledgeable and friendly, leaving you very impressed. Those are the people to talk to, but do not shove a business card in front of their face. Get to know them on a personal level, invite them to coffee, and then if it becomes appropriate, talk about their future.

Be careful with recruiters. Recruiters will bring you "amazing" candidates that are supposedly worth the 20-25% annual salary fee the recruiter demands for bringing you the candidate. In my experience, this frequently does not turn out well because that same recruiter may call that new employee in two or three years to see how "happy" they are and if they want a different opportunity. If you do think a recruiter has found someone amazing, be sure to really scrutinize their job history, including their length of time at each past employer, and speak personally with each reference provided. Be sure you understand your right to a replacement candidate or even a refund if your candidate does not work out. There are certainly some great recruiters out there; but like any business, there are also some bad eggs so proceed with caution.

Once you do have an A-player officially take your offer, your attention must be on what is the most important piece: Onboarding.

Most new employees decide in the first couple of days on a job whether they are going to stay long-term or if they made a mistake taking the role. The first few weeks of any new hire's role should be well-planned, and you should make an effort to make the new hire feel valued and appreciated. There should be a detailed schedule of what the new hire will be learning and who they will be learning from. It is also important to plan social time where the new hire can have lunch or coffee with as many different people as possible. Making the time and energy investment in your new hire in the first month will pay dividends well into the future.

One last piece of advice here: part of being an A-player is not being a jerk. No matter what you do, do not hire or tolerate jerks. I know this seems like a no brainer, but there are lots of companies that continue to employ jerks. If a C or D player is a jerk, then it is a no brainer to get rid of them. But what do you do if your biggest producer is a jerk?

Obviously, you will make every effort possible to counsel them to change their behavior; but if they don't change, get rid of them. A big producer who is also a jerk will limit your growth to only what a producer can accomplish. A jerk will chase away good people and will make other team members think it is okay to act like a jerk. They might even make you act like a jerk. This "no jerk rule" is also true, or maybe even especially true, for team members who feel they do not need to follow your rules or see themselves as being an "outsider" (not going to meetings, not attending social events, etc.). Letting go of a "big-hitter" producer or great account manager who is a jerk is hard to do, but absolutely necessary to ensure long term success and a great culture.

Chapter 17: You Can't Make Up for Bad Business with Volume

It can be hard to say no to business, especially when you are first starting to grow your agency. It can also be easy to justify writing business that you know is bad business. Perhaps the business was referred by a good client. Perhaps the business is related to your good friend from high school. Perhaps you do not know how to say no. You cannot build a great business with bad (aka unprofitable) customers. If you owned a hamburger restaurant, you could not spend $2 to make a hamburger and then sell it for a $1. That would be silly and a recipe for bankruptcy.

You may be thinking, "Tim, it does not really 'cost' me anything to sell an insurance policy. I do not have any real cost of goods to quantify, so any revenue is good, right?" But you do have costs! Every policy in your agency has an expense tied to it. You obviously have your "fixed" expenses related to your rent, E & O insurance, internet, software, account managers, reception, accounting, etc. But none of these expenses are fixed at all. More accounts mean more account managers, which means more software seats and space, which means more rent. Grow larger still, and you will need more accounting folks, an HR person, a better payroll system, etc. Remember the importance of understanding your data that we discussed in Chapter 13? Every account has a fixed cost. In my case, I found my fixed cost on each account to be around $400 in commercial lines. Anything less than $400 in annual revenue, and I was losing money on each account. This was based on my own fixed office expenses and commercial servicing expenses tied to salaries and producer commission expenses. The first thing I did when I figured this out was to stop writing accounts under $400 in revenue.

Your expense will be different. It is vital that you calculate your expenses so you know the bare minimum at which to draw the line. To help you, I created a handy little spreadsheet for you, which can be found at thebiggestleap.com.

Not writing accounts with revenue less than your breakeven point is a no-brainer, but there are other types of accounts to avoid for other important reasons.

High Maintenance Customers: When you figure out your breakeven level for the average account, that assumes the account is "average" in regard to servicing needs. If your average account needs three "service touches" per year, but a particular client requires twelve "service touches" per year, that is a problem and would need to be factored into its breakeven point.

High maintenance customers will eat up valuable time from your producers and account managers without creating additional revenue. If you do a great job, they will tell their high maintenance friends how wonderful you are, which is exactly what you do not want. If you do a poor job, they will leave, but not until giving you grief and potentially leaving a one-star review online. The only high maintenance customers worth having are those who create much higher-than-average revenue.

Business you don't understand: It sounds juicy at the time: a tech startup delivering marijuana to retirement homes via an app. Wow, exciting! The only problem is that you are not an expert in insuring tech, marijuana, or retirement homes. Walk away.

If you do not understand the business, you will be totally inefficient finding the right market to quote the risk, will be inefficient in servicing the risk, and will have created a potential E & O exposure due to handling a risk in which you are not an expert. There are only two exceptions in which to consider taking the account: (1) this account is significant enough to warrant the time it will take you to become an expert and (2) you feel this type of account will truly become a niche for you in the future. Usually neither of those items are true, so walk away.

Monoline Clients: We discussed this quite a bit in Chapter 8. Would you date someone who only wanted to give you Wednesday nights? I doubt it! Do not take on part-time clients either. You can only do a great job as an agent, and agency, if you handle all your client's insurance. Otherwise, there will be exposures left unaddressed and confusion over which policies are in place. Taking on a client's entire insurance portfolio is much better for the client and will increase your average account value, which is the biggest single determining factor in your agency's profitability.

Small Agency Bill Clients: Sure, agency bill pays you commission faster, but it is a lot more work. The amount of work that goes into agency bill accounting as you grow is incredibly significant and creates a situation where something can slip through the cracks, resulting in an E & O exposure. Agency bill should only be offered on accounts that are already profitable or where the agency bill policy is significant enough to be worthwhile.

Having many small agency bill policies will bring your office to a standstill and kill efficiency. The culprit here is usually small commercial accounts that fall into business categories that the big carriers do not have an appetite for. Often this type of client will not only be small and agency bill, but also monoline and have an unusual business description! This highlights every reason not to write an account that we just covered! Just say no!

Just like with the niche focus we talked about earlier in the book, putting this into practice is difficult because it means saying no. Practice saying no and do role play with your team on saying no to a client. The best way to say no is to make the client see the value in what you are saying. You want the monoline client to see the value of putting all their insurance with you, or the value for them to go with a specialist who is the right fit for them. Saying no the right way will expand your influence and reputation for professionalism because it is so rare.

If you are reading this book, you might be several years into building your agency already. If true, then being selective on new clients is great, but what about the massive book you have built that includes some of these "bad business" clients? You do need to make some changes with your current book if you want to be really successful.

Do not take an ax and fire every problem client we just discussed because that will cause more harm than good. You do, however, need to start somewhere. My suggestion is to start with the clients who check more than one of the problem boxes and refer them to an agency that might be a better fit as laid out below. For me, this journey started with letting go of small commercial agency bill accounts that generated less than $1,000 in total commission revenue.

I let go of these clients via a simple workflow as follows:

Step 1: Establish relationships with local independent agents who want the type of business you are looking to shed, and ensure these agents share your values of great service and great coverage.

Step 2: Run a renewal list of commercial agency bill accounts under $1,000 in commission to identify which could be let go. There are some you will have to keep because they are too close to a large VIP client or some other reason, but remember to be disciplined. In my case, I ended up letting go of about 80% of the clients on this list.

Step 3: 90 days ahead of renewal, reach out to the customer and advise you are no longer servicing businesses in their class of business. I kept it relatively vague and obviously made the language appreciative of the years of business. At the close of the email, provide the name and contact information for an agency willing to take over and ask if you are authorized to send loss runs to that agent.

Step 4: Set a reminder for 60 days out and 45 days out to ensure the account was moved to a new agent. No matter what, do not offer a renewal. It is easy to have a moment of weakness where it is easier to just renew the account, but doing that will set you back from your bigger goal.

Going through this exercise greatly improved our efficiency and average account size in our own commercial operation. We then moved onto a similar effort for rounding out monoline accounts and identifying especially service-heavy accounts.

This is not about providing less service to accounts; this is about giving appropriate service to your good customers and not overservicing the small or "low revenue/high service" customers. If you do not create these types of rules and systems, you will ultimately underservice your good customers because that second group will take up all of your resources.

I am not sure if you are familiar with the Pareto Principle. It is the concept that 20% of your actions create 80% of your results. Right now, in your agency, 20% of your accounts take up 80% of your resources; and 20% of your accounts equal 80% of your income in commercial lines. In personal lines, the numbers are actually very close, but probably closer to 70/30.

In my own agency, I found that our bottom 50% of commercial clients generated less than 10% of our commercial income! In personal lines, we found our bottom 55% of our customers generated only 20% of our personal lines income.

On the other side, in commercial lines, our top 3% of our clients generated 33% of our revenue; and our top 11% of our clients was a whopping 66% of our revenue. In personal lines, our top 20% of our personal lines clients generated 50% of our revenue. Wow! If you think that is surprising, here is the most surprising part: these numbers are also true for you!

I am so confident, in fact, that if you look at your book of business and do not see at most 30% of your clients equaling 70% of your revenue, I will personally send you a refund for the cost of this book (there is a link to request a refund at thebiggestleap.com).

Focus on adding more great clients to your book and stay away from the ones that are not so great. Make your team's life easier, create better service for your clients, increase the value of your agency, and get your sanity back.

Chapter 18: Outsourcing

For the last four years, our company has used a team of a dozen people in the Philippines for back-office support. This includes every task that our agency needs to accomplish that is not client facing. Some examples include:

- Process endorsements with carriers
- Handling carrier downloads
- Processing income email
- Pulling memos and other documents from carrier websites
- Checking payment statuses on policies
- Building proposals
- Quoting
- Remarketing... The list honestly goes on and on.

I cannot stress enough how important our overseas team members have been to our operation. When people hear the words "outsourcing," they often think of sweatshops or poorly lit call centers. For our overseas team members, this is a patently false notion. I urge you to reconsider the idea of having team members outside the United States help your organization.

There are a few reasons to look at outsourcing some back-office tasks overseas.

First and foremost, at the time this was book was written in 2023, finding team members in the United States is difficult. Because the United States currently has stagnant population growth and an almost negative birth rate, employee scarcity is likely to get more challenging in the future as opposed to easier. Finding entry-level employees to engage in relatively simple tasks like answering the phone or doing data entry can seem daunting, especially in large cities where the cost of living is high and entry level salaries are obviously low. Overseas markets present a massive pool of potential employees to pick from. At the time this book was written, our outsourcing firm had 2100 applicants for every 100 hires!

The second reason to consider outsourcing is, of course, the cost factor. A full-time employee overseas typically will cost a fraction of what an employee in the United States might cost. In addition to a lower wage, since generally you are going through another firm, you are also not paying for benefits, payroll taxes, etc. Additionally, there is far less employment law risk compared to employing a person in the States.

Lastly and most importantly, the folks you can hire overseas are just as smart, personable, capable, and amazing as anyone in the United States. With the right training and support, you can find A-players who do amazing work who are incredibly loyal and just as talented as team members you will find in the United States.

There are many firms that provide team members specialized for insurance in countries like the Philippines, Peru, China, India and more. You can go to thebiggestleap.com for more information on some of the partners we have used.

Chapter 19: Always Be Learning

I am pretty sure I am preaching to the choir here since you did buy this book and have made it this far. I just wanted to take a minute to point out the enormous number of resources that exist in this world to make you and your agency better, if you just take advantage of what is available.

I have heard many coaches say you should invest 10% of your earnings back into yourself for learning, and I agree with that advice. Some of the best ideas that are going to get you and your agency to the next level are not going to fall out of a tree and hit you in the head - you will need to seek them out.

There are a few ideas that I want to share about creating opportunities to learn and to share ideas. The first idea I will share is the idea of an Elite Lunch Group. This idea is not my own. This came from my late friend Walt Plegel, who started the first Elite Group in Orange County, CA.

The Elite Group is a group of insurance agency owners who meet monthly to discuss ideas, help solve problems, and just generally talk shop. Sure, you may be competitors, but the real threat to most agencies is online carriers and captives so there is no need to be worried about competition in these meetings. Independent agencies generally need to stick together. A typical annual agenda is available at thebiggestleap.com. I helped start my own Elite Lunch group fifteen years ago in the San Fernando Valley, and we are still going strong!

The second idea is to join a formal coaching group. I joined a CEO coaching group called Vistage several years ago. My Vistage group meets monthly to learn about an issue or topic relevant to CEOs and business owners and to help solve each other's problems. Similar groups include YPO and EO (Entrepreneurs Organization). What is great about these groups is that they are not industry specific so you can learn ideas from outside our industry. Obviously, there are also loads of networking opportunities. It is also worth checking with your local SBA office for groups and classes sponsored by the SBA at no cost to you.

Being part of this business, belonging to our local insurance industry association is also important. The big "I," or IBA (Insurance Brokers Association), has several chapters nationwide; and several other insurance industry associations populate the country. These organizations provide a great way to meet people and learn. Most importantly, these organizations lobby for our industry's best interest at the Federal and State Level.

Lastly, you should soak up information from every resource available to you, including items like this book. I do not pretend to have all the answers in this business, but I do know what worked for me. Even if you picked up just a couple of nuggets you can use, I hope this book has been worthwhile. There is such a wealth of amazing information in this world between books, YouTube, Ted Talks, etc. Anything you could possibly want to know is at your fingertips. Be a student of your craft. In this case, that means building a great insurance agency, and you will be miles ahead of the competition.

Chapter 20: If I Had To Do It All Over Again

I sold on December 31, 2021, and wrote this book a year later while continuing to run my operation, but for a much larger firm. I honestly have no regrets. Do I sometimes miss being "the big cheese?" Sure, maybe a little, but I still have the responsibility of building my team and operation so not much has really changed. Although, if I had a time machine, there *are* a few things I would go back and correct.

- <u>Producer Contracts:</u> My producer contracts did not give me first right of refusal, which meant that my producers had a ton of leverage when I sold. It turned out fine with most of the producers coming along, but it could have gone sideways just as easily.

- <u>Specialization:</u> If I built my agency from scratch tomorrow, I would pick two or three niches and focus on those; and I would only take on full-time clients within those niches.

- <u>Agency Standards:</u> We had a producer who wrote an insane amount of personal lines auto and home business, but the clients were not ideal in their claim volume. I knew this producer wrote business that ran "hot" on losses, but I figured the volume probably made up for it (I didn't follow my own advice!). This producer left with his book about a year before we were purchased; and our loss ratio fell by 20% on a book that had over $10M in premium, and this producer's book only accounted for maybe 8% of the business! Keeping this producer cost the agency millions of dollars in contingency bonuses over many years. This is not the producer's fault; this is my fault, but lesson learned. Enforce your agency standards.

- Have Fun: Over fifteen years building this agency gave me more sleepless nights than I can possibly count. I maxed out my home equity line more than once to fund the business, worried how E & O cases would turn out, lost massive accounts, lost amazing people, and often wondered if I was making the right choices for my team, customer, and company. It turns out 99% of the worry and sleepless nights were totally unnecessary.

You will lose great clients over nonsense and, unfortunately, lose great team members to competitors. You will take risks that make you lose sleep, and you will wonder if the sacrifice is worth it to get your business to the next level. **<u>In this business, the odds are stacked in your favor</u>**. This is a wonderful business. If you are honest and work incredibly hard, your success is almost guaranteed. Do not waste time worrying about the things you have no control over.

When the first business I built went bust when I was 20 years old and I ended up in bankruptcy court at age 21, the disappointment I felt as a son was worse than anything I could even imagine. So much for being a businessman. I could not even afford a sandwich.

Getting into the insurance business ultimately gave me an opportunity that no other business could offer because it really is the greatest business in the world. This industry allowed me to buy buildings with our family name on top that my Dad could drive by every day. I paid cash for my home around the corner from my Dad just 2 months before he passed away in a mountain bike accident. I am so grateful that my Dad got to see the business sell when it did for tens of millions of dollars. It was never the money that mattered. I mention the dollars only to give you a specific picture of what is possible for you.

For you, maybe money is the motivation, or maybe it is something deeper that keeps you going. For me, impressing my father was always part of the end game. I just needed to prove to my own dad I could be successful, especially after experiencing the disappointment he had with me during my bankruptcy. Now, my focus is for <u>you</u> to be successful. Whatever your motivation is to be successful, *use it*. This business gives you the best opportunity in the world to achieve every dream you have and to create your own legacy. Now get to work!

Me and my Dad, Kevin

www.ingramcontent.com/pod-product-compliance
Lightning Source LLC
Chambersburg PA
CBHW070549220526
45467CB00003B/1136